THE PHAR LAP
COLLECTION

"It's sacrilege, really, to ride other horses after being on Phar Lap"
- Jim Pike after winning the 1930 Melbourne Cup

Published by Equus Marketing Pty Ltd (ACN 058 139 898)
1/22 Summerhill Road, Glen Iris, Victoria, 3146
Tel: (03) 9889 7741   Fax: (03) 9889 7142
Web: www.pharlap.com.au   Email: equus1@bigpond.net.au
&
BAS Publishing Pty Ltd (ACN 106 181 542)
F16/171 Collins Street, Melbourne, Victoria, 3000
Tel: (03) 9650 3200   Fax: (03) 9650 5077
Web: www.baspublishing.com.au   Email: mail@baspublishing.com.au

The Phar Lap Collection
ISBN 1-920910-40-9

Phar Lap images copyright © Equus Marketing Pty Ltd
and Barbara W. Davis & Byron M. Davis

All rights reserved. No part of this publication may be reproduced, stored in a retrieval system or transmitted in any form or by any other means electronic, mechanical, photocopying, recording, or otherwise, without the prior consent of the Publishers.

The Publishers gratefully acknowledge the assistance of *The Herald & Weekly Times Limited* for supplying some of the photographs in this publication and for permitting the reproduction of *The Herald's* 1930 Melbourne Cup day report.

Design & Production
R. Kirkwood, Equus Marketing Pty Ltd.

The Publishers believe the content of this book to be true and accurate and accept no responsibility or liability for any inaccuracies.

THE
PHAR LAP
COLLECTION

A NOTE FROM THE PUBLISHER

> "He was the foal from the backblocks who became champion of the world; the tall poppy who refused to be cut down; the winner who continually beat the odds."

Phar Lap's hero status has endured for some 75 years and shows no sign of abating. Such was his grit that his spirit transcended racing. Though bred in New Zealand, the giant red horse has come to epitomise the Australian psyche. He was the foal from the backblocks who became champion of the world; the tall poppy who refused to be cut down; the winner who continually beat the odds. They changed the rules to beat him, but couldn't; on many occasions bookmakers would not set any price about him winning; and he was so invincible that trainers preferred not to run against him.

Phar Lap, better known as Big Red because of his rich chestnut, near-red color, left an indelible legacy on the racetrack - in 52 starts he recorded 37 wins, three seconds and two thirds. Included in this sequence was the unique feat of winning on each of the four days of the 1930 Flemington Spring Carnival, with a scintillating Melbourne Cup success being just one of the victories.

His story, recounted here by noted Sydney turf writer Bill Whittaker, is one of triumph and pathos. Of an unwanted, ugly young horse; the incredible bond between the horse and his strapper Tommy Woodcock; how the pair survived a shotgun ambush; the nation-wide adulation after he won the 1930 Melbourne Cup; and how the horse overcame injury to win at Agua Caliente in Tijuana, Mexico, after which he was proclaimed the best in the world.

Then there was the tragedy - his shock death, apparently by accidental poisoning, days after his international triumph. Add to this a mystery element, as it has never been determined exactly what caused Big Red's death.

Phar Lap had been a real-life hero during the times of the Depression, providing hope amidst the despair. If ever proof was needed of his popularity, you need go no further than the 1930 Melbourne Cup, when an estimated 40,000 people who could not afford to pay the admittance price to Flemington, watched the race for nothing on Scotchman's Hill, a knoll overlooking the course across the Maribyrnong River.

Even in death, Phar Lap is still a major attraction. His mounted hide is Melbourne Museum's biggest drawcard ; his massive 14lb. heart is in the National Museum in Canberra and his skeleton is displayed in the Dominion Museum in Wellington, New Zealand. But despite everything that has been written; no matter how well documented the Museum exhibits; or embellished are some latter-day versions of Phar Lap's story; until now, something has been missing. Pictorial evidence of his amazing racing career is virtually limited to the oft-repeated Melbourne Cup of 1930 and the win at Agua Caliente.

Now that has been rectified. What some consider to be the Holy Grail of Australian turf - photographs of all of Phar Lap's wins - was unearthed after a chance discussion with American Mr Dick Davis, son of Phar Lap's owner, Mr David J. Davis. Dick accepted an invitation to come to Melbourne for the opening of a new Phar Lap exhibition at the Melbourne Museum in the early 1990's.

He found it very impressive - and was further impressed by the reaction to the Phar Lap display by a visiting group of 10 to 12-year-old students. Their eager interest and knowledge of Phar Lap emphasised the special relationship between Phar Lap and the Australian people.

So it led to a visit to California with a view to researching a documentary. The Davis family checked out the attic to see what Phar Lap memorabilia lay hidden and there was certainly no shortage of material on David J. Davis' horse. There were photos, postcards and newspaper clippings. There was also a photo album, not labelled, with just a plain cover. Who knows when it was last opened?

True to the axiom of never judging a book by its cover, the album was in fact a treasure trove, containing photographs of every win by Australasia's greatest horse. Here, for the first time, was the set of photographs that turf historians had been seeking in vain for decades.

Thanks to the Davis family, they are now being presented for all to see. They dramatically enhance everything that has been written. But you have to look at them deeply. You need to absorb Phar Lap's flowing gait, his presence and his power, the ease with which he covered the ground, ears cocked wondering when he will be given his head, even though he's already lengths clear. Absorb, too, the complacency of jockey Jim Pike, on occasions looking around at daylight behind.

The collection is more than a series of race photos. It is a glimpse of Australian history, when a racehorse truly galvanised a nation. We hope that you, too, enjoy looking back on this rare moment.- **RHETT & LYN KIRKWOOD**

THE RED GIANT WHO LAPPED THEM ALL

The only way they're going to beat Phar Lap in America is if they breed a horse with wings and get Kingsford-Smith to ride him!
- Jockey Jim Pike about Phar Lap's chances after it was announced the champion would contest the Agua Caliente Handicap.

A horse, an aviator and a cricketer provided Australians and New Zealanders with a series of thrilling distractions from the heart-breaking demands of survival during the cruellest economic period of the 20th century.

The trio was barnstorming together during the worst years of the Depression, from 1929 to 1932, as though some divine force had ordered light, bright relief for millions of stressed people. Don Bradman and Squadron Leader Charles Kingsford-Smith were young Australian men; Phar Lap a New Zealand-bred horse; but such an animal that he embedded himself into the hearts and minds of almost every man, woman and child in the Southern Hemisphere. Even some 80 years years after his birth, he remains an enduring institution of the Australasian turf - an unrepeatable phenomenon!

Unbeaten at 1¼ miles (seven wins); 1½ miles (eight wins); 1¾ miles (three wins); 2¼ miles (one win), he also won four races from six starts at two miles, including the 1930 Melbourne Cup with 15 lb. (6.8 kg.) more than weight-for-age. He started favorite in three successive Melbourne Cups, the only horse in the long history of Australia's most famous race accorded that distinction. And there he stands today, in the Melbourne Museum, as the most popular exhibit; a life-like monument to his greatness. He is a folk hero and will remain so for as long as racing survives.

He became the most public horse of all time, not entirely because he was so sublime. Drama, controversy, wickedness and cruelty rode with the big, gentle chestnut from barrier to box. Criminals in Melbourne tried to shoot him on the Saturday morning before his 1930 Melbourne Cup win and finally, tragically, he suffered an agonising death in mysterious circumstances in California, USA, on April 5, 1932, when he was only a five-year-old.

Tommy Woodcock, who trained him during his short, fateful, one-race American campaign,

By Bill Whittaker

Billy Elliot ... was a very capable jockey but he had no experience in the big-time of America.

said categorically four years later in a series of articles in *The Sporting Globe* that he was offered £4,000 - an absolute fortune at that time - to give Phar Lap a "drench" (a "go-slow") the night before the 1930 Melbourne Cup, only two days after the shooting attempt failed. The offer was made by a well-dressed racing identity. Woodcock said it wasn't simple "honesty" that made him reject the offer; it was his admiration for Phar Lap. He could not have done it "for anything". When he reported the sinister news to the trainer and lessee-owner, Harry Telford, there were no recriminations - only worry. Telford admitted he had been offered £10,000 to scratch the champion from the Cup.

Woodcock said later: "From what I heard, and from a reliable source, temptation was also put in the way of (Phar Lap's regular rider) Jim Pike." (Renowned Australian jockey Edgar Britt revealed years later that Pike had in fact also been offered £10,000 to pull up Phar Lap in the 1930 Melbourne Cup, but that he had scoffed at the attempted bribe, saying he wanted only to win the race for Phar Lap's sake). Phar Lap's victory as the hottest Melbourne Cup favorite ever, and carrying 9 st. 12 lb. (62.5 kg.), bears testimony to the honesty of Messrs Telford, Woodcock, Pike and owner Mr David Davis.

In the series of articles, Woodcock also said Phar Lap was murdered, poisoned by American desperadoes in Southern California after his win at Agua Caliente.

"Human lives counted nothing to those of the doping gang and the life of a horse meant less. "They succeeded in getting at Phar Lap with the results known the world over and his death numbed me from head to foot."

Although all manner of theories abound about it, the cause of Phar Lap's death has never been clearly defined. However, Woodcock remained certain he knew those responsible for both that incident and the shooting attempt. Years later, when quizzed about Phar Lap's death, Woodcock was not so adamant. He preferred not to discuss it; he didn't want to stir the embers of controversy. Woodcock died with his secrets in 1985, never revealing the names of those he suspected, which adds more to the intrigue and mystery of the legend that surrounds Phar Lap.

However, he did debunk an assertion that Phar Lap was given tonics containing arsenic, and that the accumulated effect of these could have brought about his untimely death. Some trainers of the era used arsenic based tonics to pep up horses, but Woodcock is emphatic his charge "got nothing".

Known variously as "Big Red" or the "Red Terror", Phar Lap and the cricket genius and the fearless flyer, were all-conquering. Phar Lap was a big, plain looking, cheap-priced underdog, trained by Harry Telford, an impecunious victim of the Depression. Telford leased the horse from American owner, Mr David Davis, or, more appropriately, considering it was an era when few people owned much and the term "rent" was the operative word, Telford "rented" Phar Lap. Telford and his horse were seen as battlers, like the majority, at a time when tens of thousands regularly stood in dole queues, no doubt discussing the triumphs of Bradman, Kingsford-Smith and Phar Lap as a relief from their despair.

During 1930 in particular, these people had much to talk about when it came to sport as it was the year when Bradman thrashed the English bowlers to regain the Ashes; and Phar Lap just happened to win on each of the four days of the Flemington Spring Carnival, including the Melbourne Cup among his victories. Australia also had another sporting hero of the time, Walter Lindrum, whose skill at billiards was quickly gaining international fame.

Since then, no cricketer has equalled "The Don" and just as definitely, no racehorse - Peter Pan, Bernborough, Tulloch and Kingston Town included - has matched the "Red Terror". The clearest illustration of Phar Lap's greatness was his victory (near Tijuana, Mexico) in the Agua Caliente Handicap on March 20, 1932. It wasn't so much the win, but the way he achieved it. Phar Lap travelled by ship across the Pacific arriving in cold conditions in San Francisco; he then had an 800 km. road trip to Tijuana where conditions were boiling hot, none of which was conducive to having a horse at his peak.

Even though he had not raced since humping 10 st. 10 lb. (68 kg.) when unplaced in the Melbourne Cup the previous November, Phar Lap had to carry 9 st. 3 lb. (58.5 kg.) against some of the best horses in America and he was racing on dirt for the first time. On arrival he was starting to grow his winter coat - his body clock preparing for a Victorian winter, not a Mexican summer. A further complication occurred when he suffered a painful injury to his heel, which usually spells the end of any training program. Yet another negative factor was his rider, Billy Elliot. Capable Melbourne lightweight that he was, Elliot had no experience in the "big time" of America or on dirt tracks. Because of the hoof injury, Phar Lap's task looked even tougher when he was forced to wear heavy bar shoes for the first time.

History was also foreboding. Eight years earlier, the 1923 English Derby winner, Papyrus, who defeated Pharos (who sired turf immortals Nearco and Pharis), went to New York for a special match race against America's best horse, Zev, at Belmont Park. Papyrus, unable to cope with the dirt track and climatic changes, was annihilated by five lengths. Many American racing aficionados, remembering Papyrus, expected Phar Lap to suffer the same fate in 1932.

Phar Lap ... was a big, plain looking, cheap-priced underdog, but no horse has been able to match his ability.

How wrong they were! Papyrus was a topliner, but Phar Lap was something different again. He circled the field from last place to win easily by two lengths in track record time of 2:2.8, clipping .2 seconds from the previous best time. Despite all the obstacles, what made the victory even more meritorious was that Woodcock, in his reminiscences for *The Sporting Globe* in 1936, said that Phar Lap was not really fit that memorable day. No-one knew the horse better.

Woodcock said: "I was away from him for four days only from the day he won the Victoria Derby (November 2, 1929) until he died (Tuesday, April 5, 1932). I ate and slept with him. He went frantic if I was out of sight for a moment."

Woodcock said after Agua Caliente "Americans called him the *"Wonder Horse"*, the *"Red Terror"* and other names that lifted him high above the level of other champions. He was worthy of all the superlatives used by the Americans. Strange to say, those closely connected with Phar Lap did not employ anything but names of endearment. To Jim Pike (regular jockey) he was 'Old Boy'; to part-owner Mr D. J. Davis, he was 'the Big Fellow', but to Harry Telford and me he was just plain 'Bobby'."

The racing fraternity at large knew him simply as Phar Lap, champion of the world.

HIS BREEDING, SALE AND RACING COLOURS

Nobody could possibly have guessed or dreamed the Night Raid-Entreaty foal would become an institution, a racehorse whose unflinching courage, matchless speed and stamina would appeal to everyone.

Nature's erratic conspirators that deal so unpredictably with genetics were out in force that spring day of 1925 when imported English bay stallion, Night Raid, was mated with the black New Zealand mare Entreaty at Mr A.F. Roberts' stud farm at Washdyke, Timaru, on New Zealand's picturesque, highly fertile South Island.

It's the home of sheep, horses and resourceful people with time to think during the long, cold winters. Nobody could possibly have guessed or dreamed the resultant foal would become an institution, a racehorse of unflinching courage, matchless speed and stamina.

Imported Night Raid was a fashionably bred but third-rate horse in Sydney, the winner of a lowly Maiden Handicap at the Sydney suburban track of Canterbury Park on June 17, 1922. He had finished unplaced at his 12 previous starts in the 1921-22 season racing against moderates every time. His "reference only" resume in the 1927 Wright, Stephenson & Co's catalogue for the sale to be held in the birdcage of the Wellington Racing Club's Racecourse at Trentham, said, incorrectly, that Night Raid dead-heated for first in the Sydney Tattersall's Club's Chelmsford Stakes and he was just beginning to strike his true form and was in the middle of a special preparation for the Melbourne Cup when he broke down. The resume added (correctly):

> "Night Raid is a beautifully bred horse. His sire, Radium, is a son of Bend Or, and was a great stayer, winning among other races the Doncaster Cup, Goodwood Cup, Jockey Club Cup etc. His dam is by Spearmint (by Carbine) winner of the Derby etc....."
>
> "...Night Raid belongs to the same family as Magpie (sire of Windbag), Cicero (sire of Valais), Heroic, Syce, Lord Lyon (Derby), The Night Patrol, Traquair (sire of Woorak) etc. It would be hard to find a more attractive horse than

---

Neither Night Raid nor Entreaty were chestnut in color, yet they produced this lanky chestnut foal Harry Telford was to name Phar Lap, which meant "wink of lightning" in Singhalese.

HARRY TELFORD ...
"picked out Lot 41 because of his breeding."

Night Raid, on paper, as a prospective stud success."

Night Raid had been off-loaded to New Zealand as a sire for 600 guineas at a time when young, unproved imported stallions were worth 6,000 guineas on average. However, in his first crop of yearlings in 1927, he produced Nightmarch, a champion stayer and conqueror of Phar Lap in the 1929 Melbourne Cup. Entreaty had one run on the turf, broke down and was sold to Mr Roberts for 60 guineas. She was bred to stay being by the strong stayer influence Winkie (imp) whose son, Pilliewinkie, carried 9 st. 6 lb. (60 kg.) to victory in the 1926 Australian Cup.

Neither Night Raid nor Entreaty were chestnut in color, yet they produced this lanky chestnut foal Harry Telford was to name Phar Lap. Entreaty's first foal, Fortune's Wheel, a filly by Night Raid, showed no potential as a racehorse and was put to stud as a three-year-old without apparently being tried all that much on the track. After she had one foal and after Phar Lap's amazing success, Fortune's Wheel was put back into work in New Zealand in 1930, but once again failed to make the grade. Entreaty, who died in 1943, had 10 more foals after Phar Lap but none of her offspring possessed anything like Phar Lap's extraordinary ability.

Of her nine foals to race, only five were winners, but she was a member of a wonderful family. Her second dam, Catherine Wheel produced Treadmill (by Bill of Portland), who was the best horse of his time in New Zealand, while Entreaty's third dam, Miss Kate (imp) was not only Phar Lap's ancestress but also the ancestress of a host of topliners including the mighty Kindergarten, so there were certainly champions two and three removes back in Phar Lap's pedigree. Mother Nature merely jumped a couple of generations to give Australasia the horse of the century in a quirky display of genetics no-one can explain or fashion.

Phar Lap attracted the attention of his subsequent lessee, H. R. Telford, while he was visiting his brother Hugh in New Zealand. Telford saw the colt as a yearling and when he returned to Australia he approached many owners to induce them to buy the horse. Only Mr Davis, who until then had raced a few moderates, was interested. Alan Dexter, from the Sydney *Daily Telegraph* takes up the story:

> "After hearing Telford's opinion of the yearling he (Mr Davis) cabled to a friend in New Zealand that if he were near the scene of the sales in his travels to see Hugh Telford and bid to 200 guineas for the horse.
> The friend followed out instructions and went to the sale a little late. He made inquiries about the Lot number which the Night Raid - Entreaty youngster

represented, and found the number had been sold. Only as an afterthought did he see Telford, who informed him there were two sales that day, and the youngster was to be offered in the afternoon as the last lot of the sale.

The yearling was bought for 160 guineas and when he came to Australia, H. R. Telford leased him from Mr Davis."

New Zealand turf historians, John Costello and Pat Finnegan, in *Tapestry of Turf* say:

"Harry Telford, an ex-New Zealander and a battling trainer, picked out Lot 41 because of his breeding. Harry wrote to his brother, Hugh Telford, asking him to purchase the chestnut colt if he could buy him for less than 200 guineas.

At a sale where the top lot, Eulogy's good grandson, Honour, fetched 2,300 gns, Phar Lap was purchased for a modest 160 guineas. Harry Telford had a buyer, an American living in Australia, named D.J. Davis. But when the gangling, immature youngster arrived in Australia, Mr Davis was unimpressed and leased him to Telford for three years. Thus he gained fame in Telford's red jacket with black and white hooped sleeves."

Telford was born in Ballarat, Victoria, but during his youth in New Zealand had become a student of breeding and racing generally. The colors which attracted him were copied from a photograph of crack English jockey Fred Archer, wearing cherry, cherry and black hooped sleeves, black cap with a gold tassel, when Archer won the 1881 English Derby on Iroquois, owned by American Mr P. Lorillard. Iroquois was the first American-owned horse to win the Derby and it was fitting that 51 years later Phar Lap should carry similar colors to his triumph at Agua Caliente.

The Australian Jockey Club did not register "cherry" as a color and Telford could not have black hoops alone on the sleeves, but otherwise, apart from the gold tassel on the black cap, which wasn't allowed either, the colors are the same as those worn on Iroquois. When Telford's three-year lease expired after the autumn of 1931, Phar Lap, racing in the combined ownership of Messrs Davis and Telford, had a variation in his colors to red, green and red hooped sleeves and black cap.

> Phar Lap was purchased for a modest 160 guineas, but when the gangling, immature youngster arrived in Australia, his owner Mr David Davis was unimpressed and leased him to trainer Harry Telford for three years.

THE TWO-YEAR-OLD

The pessimists, who noted Phar Lap's height, large bones and big hooves, predicted he might make a fair jumper.

TWO-YEAR-OLD	
Starts	Record
5	1 win
	0 2nds
	0 3rds
Prizemoney £182	

Not even Harry Telford could have guessed what the future held that warm Sydney afternoon on February 23, 1929, when Phar Lap had his first start in the Rosehill Nursery Handicap over 5½ furlongs.

The pessimists, who noted his height, large bones and big hooves, predicted he might make a fair jumper. Harry Telford's trackwork rider, H. ("Cashy") Martin rode him, and the gangling chestnut, who had been gelded because Telford considered him lazy and "too smart" without thinking what his job was, did not get into the picture at any stage, finishing a poor ninth of 13 runners. A week later Phar Lap finished 8th of 16 behind Sheila, who had to survive a protest from runner-up Win's Gold, owned by Mr E.A. Haley, who 28 years later had a horse at least good enough to be mentioned in the same breath as Phar Lap - Tulloch!

At his third run, on March 16, while Phar Lap was toiling along 15th of 16 in the First Nursery Handicap over six furlongs at Rosehill, Australia's budding batting genius helped to beat England by five wickets in the final Test of the 1928-29 series in Australia. Bradman made 123 and 37 not out at the Melbourne Cricket Ground after being dropped from the Test team earlier in the series. Bradman, the "Boy from Bowral", was being feted everywhere, while the big horse who would eventually shove him off the front pages many a time in the next three years, remained a nonentity.

Despite Phar Lap's failures, Telford knew the horse was just not firing on all cylinders. "Just be patient", was his advice to Mr Davis.

Phar Lap's next race saw him run last, on April 1, 1929, this time with a new jockey, apprentice Jack Baker. On the same day Charles Kingsford-Smith had to make a forced landing in his plane the *Southern Cross* at Drysdale Mission Station in the Northern Territory during the air race to London, Baker finished last on Phar Lap over 1400m at Randwick. The winner was

Carradale, a Melbourne colt owned by L.K.S. Mackinnon, who later was to play an unpopular role in Phar Lap's remarkable career. Lachlan Kenneth Scobie Mackinnon, on the board of Broken Hill South Mining Company and chairman of the Victoria Racing Club, represented the voice of Victorian racing. His knowledge of racing was second-to-none and he raced many good horses, including the 1914 Melbourne Cup winner, Kingsburgh.

After Carradale's Randwick success, trainer Jim Scobie and Mackinnon believed Carradale could go on to win the 1929 A.J.C. Derby six months later. Little did they realise that their nemesis, the horse who would prevent Carradale winning the big Derby double at Randwick and Flemington the following spring, was right there before their eyes that April Fool's day at Randwick in 1929.

Twenty six days later, on April 27, 1929, Baker was on Phar Lap again, this time in a lowly Rosehill Maiden Juvenile Handicap over six furlongs, in which the big two-year-old gelding was to carry the feather weight of 7st. 9 lb. (48.5 kg.) with the benefit of Jack's 5 lb. allowance.

Baker recalled the win this way, some 67 years later at Rosehill: "Harry Telford told me the horse had a good chance. I was to jump him out, allow him to settle and then get going coming to the turn. I remember Telford saying 'win by as far as you can, go for your life'.

"Coming to the two furlongs the favorite Pure Tea was eight or 10 lengths in front. I was working on Phar Lap and he started to stride longer. We passed Pure Tea with about 50 yards to go and then another horse, Voleuse, gained some ground on me wide out, but Phar Lap kept going and he won by a half length.

Jack Baker's "sling" (present from connections) was £25, a very generous amount at the time and by far the best he had ever received. Baker said: "They (Telford & Co) must have known he was good, very good in fact, because their bets had to be heavy for me to be given 25 quid. A "fiver" was considered a good sling in those days." Phar Lap seemed big and strong to me on that day, but no, I had no idea he would become the best horse of all time."

As Baker said, "somebody knew" that day, as Phar Lap was very heavily backed from 20/1 to 7/1. When he was spelled near Windsor, on Sydney's outskirts in May, 1929, Phar Lap had the modest two-year-old record of one win from five starts for prizemoney of £182.

Don Bradman also went for a winter rest from cricket, after breaking a string of records for the 1928-29 season, making an aggregate 3,659 runs from 44 innings in Club, Shield and Test cricket at an astonishing 107.61 average. Charles Kingsford-Smith was oiling up the Southern Cross for further triumphs ... and tragedy.

"Phar Lap seemed big and strong to me on that day (when he won his first race), but no, I had no idea he would become the best horse of all time." - jockey Jack Baker.

THE THREE-YEAR-OLD

Telford knew plenty about good horses and he must have been certain Phar Lap was better than just "good" as an early three-year-old.

THREE-YEAR-OLD	
Starts	Record
20	13 wins
	1 2nd
	2 3rds
Prizemoney £26,794	

Phar Lap's three-year-old season left the barrier as slowly as his two-year-old days. The big, lazy, friendly gelding was no tearaway speedster, he was content to lob along at a comfortable pace.

After finishing last, eighth and 15th in his first three runs back, he lined up as rank outsider against the best horses in training in the weight-for-age Warwick Stakes over a mile at Warwick Farm on August 31, 1929. Wily Telford, a man who had travelled many a rocky racing road, knew what he was doing. He had never trained a topline galloper himself, but in New Zealand he had been stable foreman for R.J. (Richard) Mason, prince of New Zealand trainers, the man who had put the polish on hundreds of good horses, including Gloaming.

Telford knew plenty about good horses and by this time must have been certain Phar Lap was better than just "good", otherwise he would not have lined him up against stars such as Limerick, Mollison and Winalot in the Warwick Stakes. Phar Lap ran right up to Telford's expectations and more! Carrying 7 st. 6 lb. (47 kg.) (including 3 lb. overweight) Phar Lap was a fast finishing fourth behind New Zealand's crack weight-for-age performer Limerick.

At his next run en-route to the A.J.C. Derby, Phar Lap strode into second place behind top class Mollison in the Chelmsford Stakes. Jim Pike, who finished third in the race on 2/1 equal favorite Winalot, three lengths astern of Phar Lap, had a good look at Phar Lap that day. Pike, Australia's champion jockey, immediately accepted Telford's invitation to ride Phar Lap in the A.J.C. Derby. But he had no hope of reducing to the 8 st. 5 lb. (53 kg.) Phar Lap had the following week in the Rosehill Guineas, so Jim Munro got the mount and had no trouble winning by three lengths. Early signs that Phar Lap and Telford would become controversial first became evident after that race in the lead-up to the A.J.C. Derby. Back page headlines in the Sydney *Daily Telegraph Pictorial* (later *Daily Telegraph*) scolded Telford as follows:

LACHLAN MACKINNON
... his horse Carradale was runner-up again in a Derby behind Phar Lap.

FLOATS TO ROSEHILL; GALLOP IN THE DAWN
CUP AND DERBY FAVORITE'S MYSTERY TRIAL
LOST, STOLEN, OR STRAYED
Backers waited and wondered.
TRAINER TELFORD WOULD NOT TELL

The accompanying article told of a dawn float trip to Rosehill for Phar Lap to gallop with stablemate Eillom, surprising track watchers who had expected Phar Lap to work at his home track, Kensington. The paper reported:

> *"Phar Lap's (galloping) time is not known but his trial was considered highly satisfactory.*
> *On inquiries being made at the home of the gelding's lessee trainer, Mr H.R. Telford, it was ascertained Phar Lap had 'galloped at Randwick with Mooch Away.'*
> *It was also stated that Mr Telford had 'gone to Gosford races.'*
> *However, later in the day Mr Telford visited the A.J.C. offices to nominate Phar Lap for the weight-for-age races at the V.R.C. meeting. When asked where his horses had galloped, the trainer laconically replied 'Mascot', and walked away.*
> *It is hard to understand why Phar Lap was taken 14 miles yesterday to a strange track for a Derby trial,"* the paper concluded.

The stress of owning and training a good horse was starting to get to Telford who detested publicity, and never came to terms with it. Perhaps Telford was angered by a newspaper story the previous day when it was reported Phar Lap was certain NOT to run in the Melbourne Cup exactly four weeks later.

Telford said he had not invested a penny on Phar Lap for the Cup, nor had he authorised anyone to back him. The report continued:

> *"Those who had supported him, added Mr Telford, deserved to 'fall in'."*
> *Telford added he did not think Phar Lap would run two miles and even*

Officials decided to ban geldings from classic races in Sydney and Melbourne after Phar Lap won the Victoria Derby.

THE PHAR LAP COLLECTION

if he won both Derbys, Phar Lap would not start in the more important event. Even Mr D. J. Davis, owner of Phar Lap, was ignorant of the trainer's intentions. He backed his horse for a friend to win £1,000. Later the bookmaker cancelled the wager."

At a time when blocks of land in some of the better suburbs of Sydney and Melbourne were being offered for sale at £100, and a new Plymouth or Chrysler car cost £300, the 1929 A.J.C. Derby, worth £9,500 was the richest race run at Randwick. Starting 5/4 favorite, Phar Lap won under restraint by 3½ lengths from Carradale, with Honour eight lengths further astern, in a race record time of 2:31¼ a time which was to stand until Tulloch registered 2:29.1 in 1957. Honour, who was to win the NZ Derby five weeks later, had been the top-priced lot at the same Trentham sale where Phar Lap was sold so cheaply to Hugh Telford.

Don Bradman was bowling them over the same day, taking three wickets for 56 runs against Glebe and scoring 180 not out for his club side, St. George.

There was an interesting sequel to the Derby when W. (*Togo*) Johnstone was suspended for the remainder of the A.J.C. Carnival after Queen Nassau's owner, Mr T. B. McDeed, complained the young Sydney jockey had disobeyed instructions by taking the filly to a 15 lengths lead early in the race (she faded to finish last) thus ensuring a fast pace. Johnstone had resumed only a few weeks previously from a two-year disqualification for not allowing a horse to run on its merits. At that time "Togo" was a big punter, by his own admission, and so was Pike, even though betting by jockeys was - and still is - against the Rules of Racing. Johnstone's dubious tactics, against instructions, made the hard-pulling Phar Lap's job infinitely easier and he was backable at 5/4 in the Derby!

Four days later, with Melbourne's crack jockey Bill Duncan aboard (Pike couldn't ride at anything like 7 st. 8 lb., the equivalent of 48 kg.), Phar Lap thrashed Mollison in the Craven Plate.

But while Phar Lap's star was on the rise, severe hardship was only days away for Australia at large. The Wall Street crash hit on "Black Tuesday", October 29, heralding the Great Depression, causing privation and gloom for millions of people. Harry Telford and David Davis, who was entitled to a third of Phar Lap's earnings, probably had every reason not to be concerned with the looming Depression for Phar Lap had earned them the huge amount of £8,940 at the Randwick Carnival. When it is considered the *"Orient Line"* was advertising fares to England

Tommy Woodcock even spent holidays with Phar Lap who, until the day he died, would fret if he couldn't see or hear the faithful Woodcock.

"from £38" it is easy to make a comparison of just how much money £8,940 represented.

Telford declared Phar Lap a certain Melbourne Cup starter - contrary to his earlier announcement - and the veteran grandfather Bobbie Lewis was named as his Cup rider as Pike could not make his Cup weight of 7 st. 6 lb. (47 kg.).

Pike took Phar Lap to a two lengths win in race record time in the Victoria Derby with the runner-up again being Mr Lachlan Mackinnon's Carradale. Though he was old, Lewis, the rider of four Melbourne Cup winners - The Victory (1902), Patrobas (1915), Artilleryman (1919) and Trivalve (1927) - was expected to be able to easily hold the strong, relatively "green" Phar Lap behind the pace in the Melbourne Cup.

Going to the post an even money favorite - the shortest priced to that stage in the Cup's 68 year history - Phar Lap had only 13 opponents. Tens of thousands of people stopped traffic in the main streets of Sydney to listen to the "new-fangled" broadcast of the Cup to hear how the wonder horse would win the world's greatest handicap. Poor Bobbie Lewis! The race was run at a virtual "snail's pace" with Phar Lap reefing his head, wanting to go. (Oh for a Togo Johnstone on Queen Nassau!). Telford had instructed Lewis to hold the horse behind the speed and he was not about to disobey. Eventually Lewis let him go and Phar Lap was 2½ lengths clear at the three furlongs pole, but was no match for Nightmarch at the finish, with Phar Lap hanging on for third place behind runner-up Paquito.

Nightmarch, as good as he was, never again defeated Phar Lap. After the race Lewis uttered a remark he probably wished he had never made, when he said: "He (Phar Lap) pulled hard and I could not let him go with two miles in front of me. I had a good run but he could not go with Nightmarch in the straight. Had he been as good as Trivalve he would have won."

Immediately spelled, Woodcock went off on "holidays" with the big chestnut. Until the day he died, Phar Lap would fret if he couldn't see or hear the faithful Woodcock, who admitted he over-fed the champion during the summer break of 1929-30. As a result, the horse was fat and unfit when a first up third in the St. George Stakes on February 15, again with Lewis in the saddle. (It was Telford's way of putting Lewis's many critics for the Melbourne Cup defeat in their place, though Lewis did not ride him again.)

Other important sporting news was that the three young "dashers"- Don Bradman, Stan McCabe and Archie Jackson - had been selected for the 1930 English tour. Jack Ryder, the veteran Victorian, was a shock non-selection; a decision which was not overturned despite a rowdy protest meeting in the Collingwood Town Hall by several thousand Ryder supporters.

Amid a maze of speculation and side-wagers, Phar Lap was allotted 10 st. (63.5 kg.) in the Caulfield Cup and 9 st. 12 lb. (62.5 kg.) in the Melbourne Cup. Set against the weight-for-age scale, Phar Lap was rated a better four-year-old than Carbine, the greatest horse that ever lived according to the old-timers of 1930.

Squadron Leader Charles Kingsford-Smith announced he would fly the Southern Cross across the Atlantic from East to West "within five months" after which he would marry his Melbourne fiancee, Miss Powell.

Then came one triumph after another, as Phar Lap won nine races on end, with bookmakers setting no price about him in three races and putting up 10/1 on and 20/1 on about him in two other races. He was winning races by up to 20 lengths and in one of them, the A.J.C. Plate, he toyed with his Melbourne Cup foe, Nightmarch. Phar Lap smashed several time barriers in the A.J.C. Plate (2¼ miles) with jockey Elliot instructed to put pressure on Nightmarch, whom the dashing punter Eric Connolly had backed for big money. As a result, Phar Lap started at the relatively good odds, for him, of 5/2 on, with Nightmarch firming to 2/1 as Connolly sustained his betting onslaught.

Elliot took Telford to his word, sending Phar Lap along from the start, and he proceeded to provide what was the greatest display of sustained speed and stamina ever seen at Randwick.

Despite having his third run in seven days, Phar Lap ran the marathon trip in 3: 49½, cutting 4¾ seconds off the previous best time for the distance at Randwick, leaving Nightmarch 10 lengths astern.

He then went to Adelaide for two races, the Elder Stakes on May 10 and the King's Cup a week later, winning both in a canter. At the time, bookmaking was illegal in South Australia with totalisator-only betting available at the track. However, illegal Starting Price operators were doing a roaring trade - as were those in the rest of Australia - and a clever betting coup was set up in the Elder Stakes in which Phar Lap had only one rival, Fruition. *Truth* reported:

> *"With only two minutes to go before starting time it was a toss up whether backers of Phar Lap would get their money back after the (totalisator) percentage was deducted. In the last moment someone stepped in and plonked £70 on Fruition in one hit, with the result that the dividend (for Phar Lap) was only a little worse than 3/1 on.*

Phar Lap cantered home in the Elder Stakes in Adelaide.

Heavy investments were made off the course (S.P.) on Phar Lap and some bookies got a touch of heart failure when they discovered what they had to pay on the greatest certainty that ever went on a racecourse."

The actual amount put through the on-course tote was £318/15/-. Of this sum £208 was invested on Phar Lap and £110/15/- on Fruition, which resulted in the amazing dividend of £1/6/- being paid for each £1 invested on Phar Lap. The following week, against five rivals, Phar Lap paid $1/1/- for every £1 invested - odds of 20/1 on!

Phar Lap then went for a spell with his three-year-old record standing at 20 starts for 13 firsts, a second and two thirds for stake earnings of £26,794.

While he was having his winter spell, the incomparable Bradman was big news, cutting the English bowlers to pieces at Lords, Leeds and almost everywhere else. That was until another star emerged from the Darwin sky - Miss Amy Johnson. This intrepid English woman of the air had flown her plane, *The Jason,* on a long, perilous, solo flight, the first aviatrix to accomplish the feat, summarily shoving Bradman and Phar Lap off the front pages.

Other big news was that the Australian Jockey Club and the Victoria Racing Club - led by A.J.C. chairman Colin Stephen and V.R.C. chairman Lachlan Mackinnon - decided to bar geldings from major classics in Sydney and Melbourne. Their object in making such a decision was that if Australia wanted to compete on a world scale and lift standards, good colts (such as Phar Lap) should not be gelded. The decision was widely criticised and rescinded after a few years.

Despite Bradman's fighting 131 in the second innings, Australia lost the First Test at Trent Bridge on June 17, 1930, as the pundits pondered Phar Lap's Caulfield and Melbourne Cup weights. Would he get as much as Carbine, who finished second with 10 st. (63.5 kg.) in 1889 as a four-year-old? Amid a maze of speculation and side-wagers, Phar Lap was allotted 10 st. (63.5 kg.) in the Caulfield Cup and 9 st. 12 lb. (62.5 kg.) in the Melbourne Cup. Set against the weight-for-age scale, Phar Lap was rated a better four-year-old than Carbine, the greatest horse that ever lived according to the old-timers of 1930. Carbine's weight of 10 st. in the Melbourne Cup represented 14 lb. above weight-for-age, but allowing for his gelding allowance of 3 lb., Phar Lap's 9 st. 12 lb. (62.5 kg.) was 15 lb. over the scale.

Up to that stage, Patron's 9 st. 3 lb. (58.5 kg.) and Windbag's 9 st. 2 lb. (58 kg.) were the highest weights carried to victory by four-year-olds in the Cup.

While Phar Lap was already the shortest priced Melbourne Cup favorite in history, long before the race Bradman was scoring 309 not out on the first day of the Third Test at Headingly, before going on to make 334.

In the racing world, there was a hint of things to come when a report by the Melbourne correspondent of the Sydney publication *The Referee* told of :

> *"a gang of ruffians who will stop at nothing to carry out dastardly work in the nobbling of racehorses. In recent weeks four cases have been reported that leave little room for doubt about the existence of a gang that is desperate. By far the most sensational was the case of Kentle, on whom attentions of the gang centred on the day before the Grand National Steeplechase for which he was favorite at the time. At the same time an attempt was made on Mosstrooper, who next day won the National."*

The report added that deep in the night, two young men had attempted to break into the stall of Kentle, who was owned by Lachlan Mackinnon. Additionally, some poison-saturated thistle had been thrown into the box Kentle occupied the previous night.

Phar Lap had returned to Harry Telford's stables to prepare for the spring. The stage was set for the most tumultuous Spring Carnival of all time with the big, imperturbable Phar Lap the central figure in ruthless crime, huge betting, anger at his Caulfield Cup withdrawal and unequalled performances, especially at Flemington.

THE FOUR-YEAR-OLD

Jim Pike attempted to take an opening where there was insufficient room in the Warwick Stakes and, had he got through, there is little doubt Phar Lap would have won. That defeat prevented Phar Lap from establishing a record sequence of wins, which would still stand.

FOUR-YEAR-OLD	
Starts	Record
16	14 wins
	2 2nds
Prizemoney £24,671	

As Tommy Woodcock was bringing Phar Lap back to Warwick Farm to begin his four-year-old season, jockey R. Hunt made headlines after being disqualified for life for using a battery in a race at Brisbane's Ascot (Eagle Farm) racecourse. (Hunt had the audacity to ask for the battery back!)

Lachlan Mackinnon and Colin Stephen were also concerned about the evils of Starting Price bookmakers and the service given to off-course bettors by the "wireless". Stephen said: "If authorities could do something drastic that would clean up city betting it would improve matters. Not merely to benefit race clubs but from a general moral point of view.

"If this were done, then it would not matter if racing were broadcast, and wireless would remain a boon to outback followers of the turf, and to many others who are unable to attend meetings, to enjoy the advantage of hearing it over the air."

Mackinnon was emphatic Starting Price wagering had done a great deal to injure racing in Victoria. If only the pair could see racing now - the power of the TAB, the huge volume of off-course money it handles and the amazing influence of "wireless" and television.

On the cricket pitch, the bodyline "nobblers" were starting to plan ahead. It was noticed Bradman had backed away from a few Larwood bumpers and it is said the infamous "bodyline" was conceived at The Oval in August, 1930.

Phar Lap, too, was uncomfortable at his first run back in the mile Warwick Stakes, when Amounis beat him by a half head. Pike attempted to take an opening where there was insufficient room at the half mile and, had he got through, there is little doubt Phar Lap would have won, but in the end it was his lack of condition that beat him. That defeat prevented Phar Lap from establishing a record sequence of wins, which would still stand. He had won nine in a row before his spell and then won his next 14 after his first-up loss at Warwick Farm, so that

JIM PIKE ... back having armchair rides as Phar Lap kept winning races, including three in seven days.

unlucky second stopped him putting together 24 successive victories. Gloaming and Desert Gold at 19 wins, share the record for most successive wins on city tracks in Australia and New Zealand.

Jim Pike was soon back having armchair rides as Phar Lap swept all before him in races such as the Chelmsford Stakes, Hill Stakes, and the Craven and Randwick Plates. Three of the wins were over seven days and included an Australasian record of 2:3 for the 1¼ miles of the Craven Plate.

Returning to Melbourne in mid-October, Telford played "cat and mouse" with the public on whether Phar Lap would start in the Caulfield Cup. Punters kept backing him for the Caulfield handicap and the Sydney *Daily Telegraph Pictorial* reported : *"If Phar Lap sees the post he is practically certain to start the hottest favorite on record."*

It was later revealed by Woodcock that Telford had no intention of starting Phar Lap at Caulfield. He was left in the race to bluff Nightmarch's connections who decided it was a hopeless endeavour trying to match it with Phar Lap. They shipped the NZ champion back to Christchurch shortly after the Randwick Carnival, believing Phar Lap was to run in the Caulfield Cup. Well informed punters, headed by Eric Connolly, had ignored Phar Lap and Nightmarch as the first leg of the Caulfield-Melbourne Cup doubles. They concentrated on the Sydney galloper Amounis, taking him for a fortune in doubles with Phar Lap as the second leg. While Phar Lap and Nightmarch were still in the first leg, they were able to get a generous price about the Amounis-Phar Lap combination.

Bookmakers would never have laid big amounts against the pair had they realised neither Phar Lap nor Nightmarch would oppose Amounis in the first leg. It was a clever and devious betting plan.

Telford waited until the last hour before the scratching deadline to relieve Phar Lap of his Caulfield Cup engagement. Tight-lipped Telford, who rarely spoke to the media, was moved to make a statement after the uproar which followed the late Caulfield Cup withdrawal, with punters backing him almost to the hour of his scratching.

Telford said: "My lease of Phar Lap is nearly up and I would rather hand him back to his owner (Mr Davis) in good condition and see him live to be like Amounis, even if it means being misunderstood by the public. Mr Davis and I considered it was asking too much of Phar Lap to expect him to win the Caulfield and Melbourne Cups and we thought it better to give him a chance of winning the Melbourne Cup.

"There is no truth in the mischievous rumour that Mr Davis and I are on bad terms over Phar Lap and that I was over-working the horse."

A few days later, *Truth* did not spare Telford:

> *"The racing public of Australia has had some hard knocks to contend with, but none tougher than that handed out this week by H. R. Telford, lessee-trainer of Australia's champion, Phar Lap. His scratching of the Caulfield Cup favorite has made him as popular among racing men as a teetotaller at a licensed victuallers' picnic.*
>
> *Little more than 12 months ago, Telford was an insignificant man in the racing sphere; today he is more famous than popular."*

But worse was to follow. Amounis duly won the Caulfield Cup, with Mrs Maud Vandenburg, the Sydney woman who always backed Amounis, having him going for £20,000 (a colossal fortune in 1930) with Phar Lap in the Melbourne Cup. Newspapers speculated Connolly had the double going for even more.

The euphoria from favorite Amounis winning the Caulfield Cup had barely faded when four days later, on October 22, Charles Kingsford-Smith, piloting *Southern Cross Junior*, arrived in Sydney from London. About 20,000 people were at Mascot aerodrome to meet him, chanting "Smith-ee-ee, Smith-ee-ee" to the pilot who had completed the journey in the single-seater plane in 13 days.

Phar Lap's Melbourne Cup preparation was going smoothly but the Melbourne papers carried several stories of "dope-gangs" nobbling horses. "*Clifden*", writing in *The Referee* from Melbourne, gave an example of Wise Force, a former Queensland horse, who had failed badly to Amounis in the October Stakes.

> *"When the stewards decided to inquire into the poor form of Wise Force, they were met with the startling claim from the trainer (J. Accola) that the horse was doped, and a veterinary examination revealed that such was the case,"* he reported.

Amounis .... won the Caulfield Cup and was coupled with Phar Lap for a fortune in the Melbourne Cup.

This then was the atmosphere in Melbourne on W. S. Cox Plate day, October 25, 1930. The nobblers couldn't get Phar Lap because Tommy Woodcock slept alongside the horse at his Caulfield stable. Nevertheless, there were rumours galore. On Cox Plate morning, The *Daily Telegraph Pictorial* published the following three paragraph report which was a chilling warning of events to come precisely seven days later.

> *"MELBOURNE, Friday.- H.R. Telford, lessee-trainer, gave an emphatic denial today to the stories that a sensational attempt had been made during the week to injure Phar Lap.*
> *'There is not an atom of truth', he said, 'in the statement that a motor car, with number-plates covered, was driven at Phar Lap'.*
> *Telford added Phar Lap was certain to contest the W. S. Cox Plate tomorrow and Pike, who arrived from Sydney today, would ride him."*

Astonishingly, Phar Lap was shot at the following Saturday, by a person in a car with the number-plates camouflaged. Could it have been that the above report gave the criminals the idea?

Phar Lap defeated the A.J.C. Derby winner Tregilla in his customary effortless style, by four lengths, pulling up, in the Cox Plate. The Melbourne Cup was 10 days away and pundits began speculating whether "Big Red" could carry his 9 st. 12 lb. (62.5 kg.) to victory. It was noted only two horses - Malua and Carbine - had won the Melbourne Stakes (now L. K. S. Mackinnon Stakes) - Melbourne Cup double. Phar Lap had the job ahead to equal two super stars of the past. They started to compare Phar Lap seriously with the mighty Carbine, who won just about every race for his superb Melbourne trainer Walter Hickenbotham, his most notable victory being the 1890 Melbourne Cup with 10 st. 5 lb. (66 kg.) as a five-year-old in a field of 38!

One veteran racing writer, *"Martindale"*, who had seen Carbine in all of his wins at Randwick, said in *The Referee*: *"Phar Lap is winning all his races in a fashion that stamps him as*

Phar Lap wins the 1930 Cox Plate in a canter.

perhaps the greatest horse of all time".

The bookmakers who had "stood" the Amounis - Phar Lap double for a fortune were jittery. Many of them would be ruined if Phar Lap won. Like Charles Dickens' character Mr Micawber, they were waiting for something good to turn up! A disquieting story appeared in the Sydney *Sun* the day before the Melbourne Stakes.

> *"There are strong suspicions that the internal complaint which caused the death of Rigadoon, a Cup and Derby candidate who had previously been taken out of both races, was due to the effect of dope administered before he took part in the Caulfield Guineas.*
>
> *Cragford, winner of The Metropolitan, who ran fourth in the Caulfield Cup and was later scratched from the Melbourne Cup because all was not well with him, has become steadily worse. Today his trainer P. B. Quinlan, said his condition was very serious.*
>
> *Like other horses who, it is suspected, were victims of the dope fiends, Cragford* (who died shortly after) *is suffering from severe internal inflammation.*
>
> *It is believed the gang which has been operating is composed of two men and a woman."*

Then the worst incident occurred - they tried to shoot Phar Lap. It was no rumour this time. All the drama, controversy and emotion surrounding Phar Lap's late scratching from the Caulfield Cup was forgotten when it became known a couple of crooks, sitting in a car, took several shots at the champion as Woodcock led him, off a pony, back to his stable after early trackwork at Caulfield. It was Melbourne Stakes morning - Derby day at Flemington - one of the great days of racing anywhere in the world.

Tommy Woodcock gave a graphic description of the drama. He got a good view of the man who pulled the trigger of the double barrelled shotgun. In his reminiscences in *The Sporting Globe* he wrote:

> *"With the horn tooting loudly, the car swung round the corner and the driver, seeing us standing, tried to swerve into us. The car, however, had too much momentum.*

All the drama, controversy and emotion surrounding Phar Lap's late scratching from the Caulfield Cup was forgotten when it became known a couple of crooks, sitting in a car, took several shots at the champion as Woodcock led him back to his stable after early trackwork at Caulfield.

Phar Lap became excited, reared up and faced the other way about. Lucky for him he did so, as the back seat passenger poked out a double barrelled shot gun and fired point blank. The pellets were embedded in the picket fence where Phar Lap had been standing.
The shooter had the lower portion of his face covered with a handkerchief but it dropped as he fired and I got a second view of him. I could pick him out of a million.
I nearly dropped in my tracks with surprise when I saw him on a racecourse some months later and found out who he was!"

TOMMY WOODCOCK ... almost dropped in his tracks when he saw the person who tried to shoot Phar Lap on a racecourse some months later.

Reading between Woodcock's lines, it is almost certain the gunman was very well known and possibly respected on Victorian racetracks; a man who had a lot of money at stake in what were desperate times.

Adding to the drama, it was revealed years later by renowned Australian jockey, Edgar Britt, that he had it on good authority Jim Pike rejected a £10,000 offer to stop Phar Lap from winning the Melbourne Cup. This was a fortune in 1930; sufficient to buy a four bedroom home in the best suburbs of Sydney or Melbourne. The offer, which did not even tempt honest Pike, was made by the successful trainer Mick Polson (a knockabout punter) who was a close friend of Pike. Edgar Britt was indentured to Polson at Moorefield and Randwick during the early 1930's and once rode two winners for the Telford stable on one day at Flemington.

Britt, now in his early 80's, recalled the scandalous background to Polson's reluctant chat with Pike on 1930 Cup eve during a long video-taped interview with Sydney journalist David Kennedy, which has been marketed as *"Britt: Aces and Kings of the Turf."* Britt told Kennedy that some 20 years after the 1930 Melbourne Cup, while he was home on holidays after riding in England, Polson revealed to him that he was asked to see Pike on behalf of a consortium which was aware of his close friendship with Pike. Polson told Britt he knew what Pike's answer would be, but he promised he would put the "question" even though he hated doing it.

Polson said he had been asked to remind Pike 10,000 "quid" was a fortune, that he (Pike) was getting on in years and the huge bribe would set him up for life. Britt told Kennedy: "What he (Pike) told them to do with the money, I wouldn't like to say here. Jim told my old boss (Britt always refers to Polson as his "old boss") that he didn't give a damn about getting old, or the money. All he wanted to do was win the Cup on Phar Lap."

Kennedy to Britt: "Who was behind the offer Edgar?"

Britt: "I don't know. It wouldn't all be bookies; some would be big gamblers."

Woodcock admitted he had been offered £4,000 to "stop" Phar Lap by giving him a drench the night before the Cup. Woodcock said he knew Telford and Pike had been offered more. Never had a horse been asked to overcome such sordid villainy to win a race.

Thus Phar Lap became the most guarded racehorse in Australian history, being taken to Flemington for the Melbourne Stakes with an escort of six motor cycle policemen. They accompanied him from the enclosure to the course proper and just kept out of the reach of his heels until he went down the track for his race.

After he won the Melbourne Stakes by three lengths, he was hurried back into his float and taken back to Caulfield, though the race hardly rated a mention, being "lost" in the shooting scandal copy.

Mr Davis, owner of Phar Lap, declared: "I have no doubt it (the shotgun incident) was intended to kill the horse. The trouble is ante-post betting. No matter how low a man is, it is strange he should want to shoot a beautiful animal like Phar Lap. If he gets to the course Phar Lap will win the Melbourne Cup."

Mr Davis and Telford decided to whisk the champion away from Caulfield, leaving a big chestnut hurdler in his place in his stall. Late on the Saturday night, in high secrecy, Woodcock and Phar Lap were floated to Mr Guy Raymond's St. Albans Stud near Geelong, where Phar Lap would round off his preparation in reasonable privacy.

Harry Telford told the press by phone on Sunday night that "Phar Lap will win the Melbourne Cup without an effort. Some people who know he is a good thing for the race have become desperate in their attempt to prevent him from getting to the post. The public can be assured I will take no risk of anyone doing damage to the horse between now and the time he steps on the course at Flemington."

Tommy Woodcock slept alongside Phar Lap at St. Albans and the champion was out for exercise on Cup morning at Geelong racecourse with jockey Bobby Parker atop and Woodcock alongside on one of Mr Raymond's horses.

Stan Boyden's motor float proved hard to start on Cup morning and there was some panic before it eventually spluttered into action and Phar Lap was on his way to Flemington, escorted by two police motor cycle patrols - one in front and the other behind the float. A wireless patrol car also joined in to make sure the horse arrived safely.

Mr David Davis ... "If he gets to the course Phar Lap will win the Melbourne Cup."

Phar Lap became the first and only horse to this day to start at odds-on in the Melbourne Cup and no four-year-old before or since has been able to win with anything near his weight of 9 st.12 lb. (62.5 kg.).

No sporting hero, certainly no mere horse, has made such a melodramatic, theatrical entrance to a sporting arena anywhere in the world. Really, it was unnecessary - especially at Flemington - where the crowd would have torn to shreds anyone who attempted to harm the public idol. Earlier, at Caulfield, all manner of deceptions were used to hide Phar Lap's whereabouts. Harry Telford even dressed up another horse in Phar Lap's gear and worked him as "Phar Lap" in front of the media at Caulfield.

Phar Lap's dashing Melbourne Cup win was an anti-climax. He simply coasted to victory by three lengths. In so doing, he became the first and only horse to this day to start at odds-on in a Melbourne Cup; and no four-year-old before or since (including Carbine) has been able to win with anything near his weight of 9 st. 12 lb. (62.5 kg.)

Don Bradman arrived home in Bowral after his long Ashes tour the day Phar Lap won the Cup, and on a sad note, Charles Kingsford-Smith agreed to his father William's last request, to spread his ashes into the Tasman Sea.

But the 1930 V.R.C. Spring Carnival had not ended for Phar Lap. Two days later he came out on Oaks day to win the Linlithgow Stakes (one mile) in a breeze. Even then he wasn't finished. On the Saturday only two other rivals would race against him in the C.B. Fisher Plate (1½ miles) which he won by 3½ lengths. Over the four days of the Carnival he had won four races: The Melbourne Stakes (1¼ miles); the Melbourne Cup (two miles); Linlithgow Stakes (one mile) and the C.B. Fisher Plate (1½ miles) - all of them in a canter. He raced a total of 5¾ miles "without getting out of second gear", as Pike put it. His onslaught that Flemington spring remains unmatched.

While Phar Lap was spelling, Mr Davis received the following cable from a London newspaper: *"Phar Lap considered here superior to Carbine. Widespread demand to see him race. Would you issue a world challenge to race him at Ascot?"*

Mr Davis replied: *"Will race any horse you send over here, any distance, any amount!"*

Nothing came of the challenge!

When weights were issued for the big autumn handicaps, Phar Lap was given a mammoth 10 st. 13 lb. (69.5 kg.) for the Sydney Cup, on a 6 st. 7 lb. (41.5 kg.) limit and the V.R.C. Handicapper, Mr J.H. Davis, gave him 11 st. 1 lb. (70.5 kg.) in the Newmarket, also on a 6 st. 7 lb. (41.5 kg.) limit. His Sydney Cup weight was 30 lb. more than weight-for-age for a four-year-old gelding, the heaviest weight given a horse in the Sydney Cup and 5 lb. more than The Barb's 10 st. 8 lb. (67 kg.) which he carried to victory in 1869.

THE PHAR LAP COLLECTION

His Newmarket weight was not a record; the great New Zealander Machine Gun received 11 st. 3 lb. (71 kg.) in 1906 when he finished unplaced behind Pendant. Although Pike said he could win both races, Messrs Telford and Davis withdrew the champion from the handicaps to concentrate on weight-for-age races. Soon after, the V.R.C., led by Lachlan Mackinnon, dropped a bombshell. They announced alterations to the weight-for-age rules at Flemington. These changes, aimed at stopping Phar Lap having "trot and canters" came at a time when the V.R.C. was in a poor financial situation. Attendances had dropped despite the presence of the super horse and betting at the track was suffering as punters stayed away from the course to bet with illegal Starting Price operators.

The Flemington onslaught of 1930

Date	Race	Distance	Won by
Saturday, November 1	Melbourne Stakes	10 furlongs	3 lengths
Tuesday, November 4	Melbourne Cup	2 miles	3 lengths
Thursday, November 6	Linlithgow Stakes	1 mile	4 lengths
Saturday, November 8	C.B. Fisher Plate	1½ miles	3½ lengths

The V.R.C.'s savage weight-for-age alterations provided for a 7 lb. penalty for all horses who had won a weight-for-age race worth £1,000 to the winner; the deletion of the 3 lb. allowance to geldings; and the inclusion of a 7 lb. allowance for three-year-olds and 14 lb. for horses aged four and over, who had won neither a weight-for-age race worth £500 nor a handicap of £1000 to the winner.

By this time, Harry Telford had bought a half-share in Phar Lap for £4,000 at the expiration of his three-year lease from Mr Davis. The £4,000 for a half share in such a great horse seemed cheap, but it was stipulated Mr Davis was able to take Phar Lap to America if he so desired. While the lease was in existence, Phar Lap had won £46,847 of which Harry Telford received £31,298 and Mr Davis £15,549. Huge money!

Harry Telford claimed the V.R.C. would never have introduced the penalties if the best horse was owned by a "silvertail", but *The Referee* defended Mackinnon and his committee. The widely respected sporting paper declared on February 25, 1931, that:

"The V.R.C. was widely condemned for altering the conditions of its autumn

weight-for-age races, but with a champion like Phar Lap completely overshadowing his probable opponents, there was an excuse for taking a step that might add a little interest to those events.

Despite his penalty and the allowance received by some of the others, Phar Lap is a certain favorite for each weight-for-age race in which he runs...."

Phar Lap resumed with a first up win in the weight-for-age St. George Stakes and then humped a 20 lb. penalty on a damp track to win the weight-for-age Futurity Stakes with 10 st. 3 lb. (65 kg.), which Pike claimed to the day he died was the gamest effort of any horse he had ridden.

In March 1931, Harry Telford, by now a household name in Australia, announced he was "branching out" and his young strapper, Tommy Woodock, would take over stables he intended to establish in Sydney. Telford would remain at his richly appointed Melbourne establishment at Braeside, where he had a private training track. Woodcock was to train horses at Randwick largely for one of Telford's wealthiest Sydney clients, who raced horses under the assumed name of "Mr Smithden". The A.J.C. granted Woodcock, then only 25, a No. 1 trainer's licence, making him almost certainly the youngest person ever to get a No. 1 trainer's licence at Randwick. However, the plan did not come off and Woodcock, so vital to Phar Lap's well-being, stayed with the champion in Victoria.

Phar Lap continued his winning way in the Essendon Stakes on February 28, 1931, when a little known South Australian trainer, one J.M. Cummings, owned and trained the last winner, St. Mary. Jim Cummings' three-year-old son, James Bartholomew (Bart) was barely out of nappies, yet years later he was to become a record-holder at Flemington, by training 11 Melbourne Cup winners up to 2005. Four days later Phar Lap achieved his 14th successive win by taking the King's Plate. The following day the then Sydney *Daily Telegraph* turf writer, *"Cardigan"* (Bert Wolfe), who was to become Racing Editor of the *Melbourne Herald*, wrote:

"There are persistent rumors that Phar Lap, the best horse the Australian turf has seen since the days of Carbine, may go to America

The King's Plate ... win No. 14 on end.

to race. Mr D. J. Davis, part-owner of Phar Lap, when spoken to last night on the telephone in Melbourne, said he had made no plans and at present the possibility of Phar Lap going abroad to race was remote.

If Messrs Davis and Telford did have intention of sending Phar Lap to America, no doubt they would concentrate on the great racing Carnival which is held by the Agua Caliente Jockey Club, a few miles across the border in Mexico from California. During this meeting on March 22 the second renewal of the $100,000 (£28,000) Agua Caliente Handicap, the world's richest race, will be held."

> "Phar Lap resented being loaded on to the float that day and on the way to Flemington he was sick and trembling. When I got out, Telford was waiting with his saddle. I told him the horse was too ill to run.

The extremely astute, young and keen *"Cardigan"*, was correct in almost every detail. The American trip was 10 months away!

At this time, early March, 1931, a minor miracle occurred at the Sydney Cricket Ground. Don Bradman was dismissed for a duck playing in the fifth and final Test of the 1930-31 series against the West Indies. Bigger shocks were ahead. Four days after Bradman's duck, the mighty Phar Lap was beaten in the C. M. Lloyd Stakes - after having won 14 races on end. *"Cardigan"* sprang to Phar Lap's defence.

"No doubt the V.R.C. Committeemen who originated the idea of tinkering with the conditions of standard weight-for-age races run at Flemington were highly delighted at the result of the Lloyd Stakes.

They will possibly imagine that Waterline's defeat of the champion justified their action. To most people it will be just the reverse."

Waterline, carrying 14 lb. less than weight-for-age defeated Phar Lap, burdened with 7 lb. more than weight-for-age, by a neck. Woodcock claimed it was not the weight which prevented Phar Lap from winning, it was just that Phar Lap was "tired, jaded and ill" that day.

"When I started to dress him for his journey in the float to Flemington that day, he commenced to snap at me, as much as to say I should know better," Woodcock said.

"Phar Lap resented being loaded on to the float that day and on the way to Flemington he was sick and trembling. When I got out, Telford was waiting with his saddle.

"I told him the horse was too ill to run. I drew attention to the way he was sweating. Telford told me I had too heavy a rug on him."

Some time that afternoon, the airliner *Southern Cloud,* carrying eight people, disappeared en-route from Melbourne to Sydney. A total of 22 search planes and thousands of people on foot searched the rough country in northern Victoria and southern NSW looking for the aircraft, with Air-Commodore Kingsford-Smith being among the search pilots. "Smithy", himself to be lost forever in a later plane crash, never did find the *Southern Cloud* which was not discovered until 27 years later, in 1958.

Phar Lap was back in the news on June 29, 1931, when weights were declared for the Caulfield and Melbourne Cups. "Big Red" had 10 st. 11 lb. (68.5 kg.) at Caulfield and 10 st. 10lb. (68 kg.) in the Melbourne Cup. Carbine's weight-carrying record for the Melbourne Cup was the 10 st. 5 lb. (66 kg.) he humped to victory as a five-year-old in 1890. The Handicapper, Mr J.H. Davis, rated Phar Lap 5 lb. better than Carbine, thus creating a flood of comment at the time as Carbine was revered by many who had seen him win 41 years earlier. *"Cardigan"* wrote in the Sydney *Daily Telegraph:*

> *"Champion as Phar Lap has proved himself to be, it is unlikely he will prove equal to the task. It is a tremendous impost, and probably his owners will reserve him for weight-for-age races."*

At the end of his four-year-old season Phar Lap had the amazing record of 16 starts for 14 wins and two seconds in 1930-31, his victories including the Melbourne Cup with a record weight for a four-year-old that stands to this day.

Handicapped at 10 st. 10 lb. (68 kg.) in the Melbourne Cup, Phar Lap was required to carry 5 lb. (2 kg.) more than Carbine had when he set the weight-carrying record in the 1890 Cup; thus Phar Lap was considered by the Handicapper as a better horse than Carbine.

THE FIVE-YEAR-OLD

"Well, the ballyhoo was no dream. A great racehorse, termed the 'Terror of the Antipodes', came 10,000 miles from kangaroo land, made his American debut with a reputation excelled, perhaps, by no thoroughbred, unless you wish to argue Man O'War, and today proved himself a runner that can be regarded as the greatest any Agua Caliente attendance has ever seen."

FIVE-YEAR-OLD	
Starts	Record
10	9 wins
	0 2nds
	0 3rds
Prizemoney £4,778 + US$50,000	

By August 1931, Phar Lap was back in work at Braeside where Telford and Woodcock were preparing him in the privacy of Telford's own track.

Nobody except Woodcock knew how fit Phar Lap was the day he resumed in the Underwood Stakes over a mile at Williamstown (Melbourne) on August 25, 1931. Telford had kept telling the press Phar Lap was unfit; that he had been unable to give the champion any worthwhile work due to continuous rain. When the Williamstown meeting was postponed from Saturday to Tuesday, due to the rain, Pike, who had travelled to Melbourne by train to ride Phar Lap, decided to go home. Telford informed him Phar Lap was not fit and could get beaten.

Woodcock, who knew Phar Lap much better than Telford, pleaded with Pike to stay, for he considered Phar Lap was fit enough, knowing full well the work he had given him at Sol Green's Underbank Stud at Bacchus Marsh during April, May and June. Tommy failed to persuade Pike who caught the next train home to Sydney.

So, with Billy Elliot aboard, Phar Lap proved Woodcock right, winning the Underwood easily by 1¾ lengths from his stablemate filly, Rondalina. Betting on the race was remarkable, with Phar Lap drifting in the market from 5/4 to 2/1, while Waterline, who finished fourth, was at 9/4. The 2/1 was Phar Lap's longest price since he had won the Rosehill Guineas - also at 2/1 - in September, 1929.

The continuing effect of the Depression on racing was emphasised at the A.J.C.'s 1931 Annual General Meeting when chairman Stephen announced a disturbing loss of £26,367 for 1930-31. Racing revenue for the year dropped by £75,233 and instead of making the usual £10,000 profit on the Spring Carnival the A.J.C. lost £7,000, despite the fact prizemoney had been reduced by 32 per cent. Further proof of the financial doldrums was the prizemoney for the A.J.C. Derby would be reduced from £8,000 to £5,000.

However, the Spring Carnival in Sydney was the mission for Phar Lap after he cantered home by 3½ lengths in the Memsie Stakes at Caulfield. Telford announced the turf idol was to contest weight-for-age races there before deciding his Melbourne spring commitments. Returning to his old stamping ground, Rosehill, Phar Lap had his usual trot and canter to win the Hill Stakes from only three rivals.

Phar Lap was shoved off the main sporting pages the following week when Ambrose Palmer, from Footscray, Melbourne, came to Sydney to win the Australian middleweight championship from Sydney boy, Bob Thornton, at the Stadium. Palmer was watched by his wife of one week as he scored a comfortable points decision over Thornton, who won the crown on a foul from Palmer a few weeks previously.

Like the A.J.C., the NSW government was also facing financial difficulties, so Premier J.T. Lang put a lot of noses out of joint by announcing that he - and not Royalty - would cut the ribbon for the opening of the Sydney Harbour Bridge the following March. As the government was "broke" Lang claimed he was saving £30,000 by not inviting the Prince of Wales or the Duke of York for the opening ceremony!

Harry Telford, meanwhile, was not revealing plans at all. He would not declare whether Phar Lap would run in the Caulfield Cup, the Melbourne Cup - or both - with the result that *"Cardigan"* wrote in the *Daily Telegraph*:

> *"If Edgar Wallace lived in Australia he could write a mystery story concerning the spring mission of Phar Lap. His connections are still silent as to whether he will run in either of the Cups."*

Pike had his usual armchair ride on Phar Lap to win the Spring Stakes on Derby Day, completing a treble for New Zealand breeding, with Dominion-bred Amon Ra and Autopay winning the A.J.C. Derby and the Epsom Handicap. Phar Lap backed up four days later to win the Craven Plate over 1¼ miles in a sizzling 2:2½, thus breaking the 2:3 Australian record he had set in the same race the year before.

Another record bid failed when Charles Kingsford-Smith arrived in London unable to beat J.A. (Jim) Mollison's time of eight days, 19 hours and 40 minutes after setting out for London from Wyndham in Western Australia.

Armchair ride for Pike in winning the Spring Stakes.

On the sporting front, Phar Lap's owner, Mr Davis, said Phar Lap would not run in the Caulfield Cup and was by no means a certain starter in the Melbourne Cup, while at Coogee Oval on Saturday, October 10, Australia's "run machine" Don Bradman scored a superb 246 for his club side St. George against Randwick. "The Don" scored his last 100 in only 66 minutes, obviously working at a much faster rate than Phar Lap, who "trotted" the two miles of the Randwick Plate that afternoon against one opponent in 3:31.

A young apprentice, who was to ride years later for the King of England, rode in another race that afternoon. Edgar Britt was unplaced that day at Randwick, but still well remembers Phar Lap and his jockey, Jim Pike, whom Britt says was a "genius" in the saddle; a gifted jockey who could coax the best from all horses without using the whip.

"He had very large hands, long arms and neck and relatively short legs, though he was a lot taller than most jockeys," Britt said. "He had a great habit of getting his horse to 'lean' on yours in the straight without really causing a bump. He was clever and skilled; surely one of the greatest jockeys of all time."

As Phar Lap was back in Melbourne, preparing for the Spring Carnival, one of Sydney's most respected racing writers, Alan Dexter, again came out in favour of the V.R.C.'s penalties and allowances idea, after watching Phar Lap canter to three successive wins at Randwick. Dexter wrote in the *Daily Telegraph*:

> *"If the A.J.C. hopes to maintain interest in its weight-for-age races it will have to make drastic alterations, and although extensive opposition would arise, it would be beneficial to racing if the recent V.R.C. swing towards penalties and allowances were followed.*
> *It would sound the death-knell of standard weight-for-age, but that would be better than reducing racing to little more than a farce, and that, more or less, is what weight-for-age events have proved in the last couple of years. Phar Lap's part-owner, H.R. Telford, has complained bitterly about the altered weight-for-age conditions in Melbourne but, after all, he has had a fair innings, and surely he does not begrudge another horse being given a sporting chance of beating his great champion."*

The penalties and allowances were quickly forgotten once Phar Lap was in America!

Such was Phar Lap's dominance at weight-for-age, journalist Alan Dextrer wrote: "If the A.J.C. hopes to maintain interest in its weight-for-age races it will have to make drastic alterations, and although extensive opposition would arise, it would be beneficial to racing if the recent V.R.C. swing towards penalties and allowances were followed."

> *In a bid to goad the connections of Phar Lap to run in the Melbourne Cup with a massive 10 st. 10 lb. (68 kg.), Lachlan Mackinnon said that Carbine, and not Phar Lap, was the best horse he had ever seen; in fact Carbine was the best horse the world had ever seen!*

The author was given access to A.J.C. Committee Meeting Minutes for the relevant period during 1931 when the V.R.C. made its controversial weight-for-age changes, but at no stage was it discussed at Committee level by the A.J.C., which must have been prepared to maintain the status quo. One point of discussion, however, was whether the A.J.C. would buy a house from Jim Pike in Doncaster Avenue (adjacent to Randwick racecourse) only to decide against the purchase because, in their view, Pike was asking "too much" - £1,000.

Phar Lap's first race in the Melbourne spring was to be the W.S. Cox Plate (thus he missed the Caulfield Cup as predicted by Mr Davis). As Woodcock and Telford were putting the finishing touches on Phar Lap's preparation, neither Harry Telford nor Mr Davis would confirm whether the "Red Terror" was a certain Melbourne Cup starter, and bookmakers were complaining that they couldn't do any pre-race business on the Cup because nobody knew Phar Lap's program.

On Cox Plate morning, Mr Davis announced Phar Lap would run in the Cup, provided the track was reasonably good. Phar Lap's effort that afternoon in the Cox Plate was a great prelude to Flemington. *Truth* reported the victory in the following colorful terms:

> *"With Pike hanging on to him and refusing to let him stretch out, Phar Lap led down the side and although he was bounding along like a big red kangaroo and kept flicking his ears back and forth like a playful hare, he still had too much foot for the rest of 'em."*

Mr Davis collected the Cox Plate trophy - a small loving cup of solid gold - this being the first trophy he had received, as Harry Telford, the lessee-owner had collected all the others. Mr Davis told the media after the Cox Plate: "Usually when part-owners win a trophy they toss for its possession, but Harry told me yesterday that if Phar Lap won he would like me to have the Cup. This year I am coming into my own and of course the trophy will always be a treasured possession."

"Big Red" had now won £55,925 - an Australian record by a "mile"- and had moved to fifth place on the world's greatest stake-winners' list. Those in front of him were the Americans Sun Beau, Gallant Fox and Zev and the crack English horse Isinglass who had won £57,455. But it was Phar Lap's record Melbourne Cup weight of 10 st. 10 lb. (68 kg.) that was more of a talking point after the Plate.

V.R.C. chairman Mackinnon said the weight would not stop him. He said: "My view is it will not hurt a five-year-old gelding like Phar Lap in the slightest degree to carry his allotted weight. If he does not compete in events like this, what is the use of keeping him merely for weight-for-age races?" He added Carbine, and not Phar Lap, was the best horse he had ever seen; in fact Carbine was the best horse the world had ever seen!

With the Cup a week away, Phar Lap was 7/4 to win; bookmakers were taking no risks, regardless of his weight. Bobbie Lewis, who was still riding at the age of 53, and who rode Phar Lap in his 1929 Cup defeat, said he doubted Phar Lap could win with such an impost.

It was "The Don" who made the main sporting news on Derby eve, when he rejected a lucrative offer to play for Accrington Club in England - he had instead accepted offers from Associated Newspapers *(The Sydney Sun)*, Radio 2UE and F. J. Palmer and Son stores in Sydney. Cricket's batting wizard was not being paid to play cricket, the game being tied to amateurism, but rather he would do writing, broadcasting and promotional work.

Phar Lap won the Melbourne Stakes easily enough on Derby Day but bookmakers sensed something was amiss. They wanted to "lay" him for big amounts in the Cup. Pike was to say later that even though he won the Melbourne Stakes without being ridden out, Phar Lap had nothing in reserve in beating Concentrate by a mere half length. Tommy Woodock also realised the champ was tired coming into the Melbourne Cup. In his memoirs, Woodcock wrote:

> *"I told Jim (Pike) that to my mind it was ridiculous to start Phar Lap and asked him to take care of him in the race.*
> *"Don't worry, old son, I won't knock your pal about', came Pike's reply."*

Woodcock and Telford knew Phar Lap had virtually no hope with 10 st. 10 lb. (68 kg.) on Cup day, even though there was no rain and the track was perfect. Pike was on a high, having won the Derby on Johnnie Jason, his fourth successive win in the major Flemington classic, and his sixth success since he first won on Beverage in 1910. Yet Pike must have been worried as he took Phar Lap to the post for the Cup after hearing Woodcock's plea not to knock him about.

As predicted by Woodcock, Phar Lap was well below his best and could finish only eighth behind White Nose, the horse Pike had tipped as his biggest

Phar Lap "bounded along like a big red kangaroo flicking his ears back and forth like a playful hare".

Lachlan Mackinnon ... rumoured to have warned Phar Lap's connections the day before the Cup that unless they started the horse, the Committee would take serious action.

danger in a newspaper article the day before. White Nose, with only 6 st. 13 lb. (44 kg.) led all the way, apart for a brief period in the middle stages where he shared the lead. Phar Lap had moved to sixth at the half mile but it was under sufferance and he lost ground in the last furlongs.

Phar Lap had started at the good price of 3/1, but Pike said he was beaten at the half mile; he had no zip and as a result he had treated Phar Lap sympathetically in the home straight. Telford said after the race he had again sought police protection for Phar Lap on Cup day, due to threats that two Sydney "desperadoes" would fire darts impregnated with poison at Phar Lap. For this reason, the Clerk of the Course was requested to ride on the near side of Phar Lap as he was taken up the lane to the mounting yard.

It was freely rumoured in Melbourne the day after the Cup that the V.R.C. chairman Mackinnon had warned Phar Lap's connections the day before the race that, unless they started the horse, the Committee would take serious action. *"Cardigan"* wrote:

> *"However, it is impossible to confirm the story, but L.K.S. Mackinnon did say on Cup eve that the public had to be protected."*

Phar Lap was declared a starter for the C.B. Fisher Plate four days later but was withdrawn on the morning of the race. Rumours quickly spread that he was "definitely going to America". Veteran Melbourne trainer Dick Bradfield, who had prepared numerous imported horses in the past, warned there were risks involved if the horse left our shores. His advice to Messrs Davis and Telford was chillingly accurate: "I have no doubt Phar Lap would stand the trip to Mexico, but, considering all the risks involved, I think he is safer in Australia."

Even though the trip had not been confirmed, Pike declared he would not go to America.

While this news was raging, a cricket "miracle" occurred in Brisbane where the fast bowler Eddie Gilbert had Bradman out for a duck in the Queensland - NSW match. The NSW Sheffield Shield manager, Mr A.L. Rose, caused a sensation by declaring that Gilbert was a "thrower" and four NSW players said privately every ball Gilbert delivered to Bradman was a throw.

Nine days after the Melbourne Cup, Phar Lap was declared a certain starter at Agua Caliente for a Handicap worth US$100,000 (reduced by half once Phar Lap arrived in America). Soon after it was announced that Billy Elliot would ride him and that Tommy Woodcock had agreed to train him because Harry Telford declined to go. Phar Lap was shipped to New Zealand on the first stage of his American adventure in early December, 1931. He holidayed with Woodcock at Hugh Telford's Trentham stables until December 29 when he was loaded aboard the *S. S. Monowai,* bound for San Francisco.

Phar Lap was to be given every comfort a horse could have, his "cabin deluxe" was 15ft. square and had padding nearly a foot thick. It was built so that on rough days he was protected from driving spray and on warm days he was able to enjoy the fresh air. He also had an exercise "yard", the same size as his "cabin" and capable of holding 12 tons of sand. These two areas were connected by a railed-off path of matting tacked on the deck and liberally covered with sawdust to prevent him slipping.

Weights for the Agua Caliente Handicap were issued early in January and *"Cardigan"* commented in the *Daily Telegraph* that his 9 st. 3 lb. (58.5 kg.) had taken care of him but was not harsh. Phar Lap arrived safely in San Francisco and was then taken 800 km. by motor horse float to Tijuana, arriving on January 28, 1932, in good time for the race which was to be run over 1¼ miles on March 20. Mr Davis employed the Cessnock (NSW) veterinary surgeon Bill Nielsen to care for Phar Lap and assist Woodcock while trackwork rider Jack Martin rode Phar Lap in his work. Everything was going to plan until Phar Lap split his hoof 10 days before the race. *"Cardigan"* was on hand to cover the race and despatched copious copy on the champion's hoof injury, which was injected with a local anaesthetic and fitted with a bar shoe.

Mr Davis, who was in San Diego, had assured race officials Phar Lap was certain to run. Woodcock recalled Mr Davis had backed the horse heavily with bookmakers at Agua Caliente and "in many other places" off the track.

Billy Elliot was confident. He told a radio audience in America he would jump into the Tijuana river with the saddle tied around his neck if Phar Lap didn't win!

The Depression was at its worst but there were two exciting diversions for Australia on the weekend of March 19-20, 1932. Phar Lap was to race in Mexico on the second day, while the Sydney Harbor Bridge was to be opened by Premier Jack Lang on Saturday afternoon, March 19. It had taken more than 100 years for the bridge to become a reality, the first suggestion of it having been made by Governor Macquarie's architect, Francis Greenaway, in 1816. But a man riding a broken down racehorse stole the show from Lang.

Captain F.E. De Groot, wearing military uniform, rode on to the bridge and pierced the symbolic opening ribbon with his sword before Premier Lang could officially cut it. De Groot had simply joined the Vice-Regal guards-in-saddle a couple of hours before the big event.

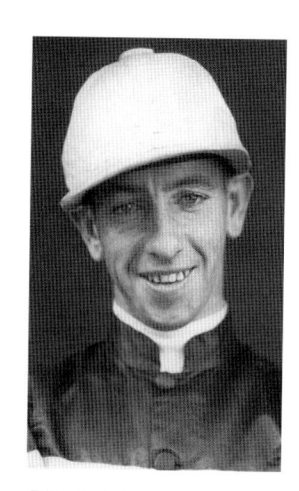

Billy Elliot ... was so confident of winning the Agua Caliente Handicap that he said he would jump into the Tijuana River with the saddle around his neck if Phar Lap didn't win.

Arrested, De Groot was proclaimed "perfectly sane" by doctors and was subsequently charged with "maliciously damaging a ribbon valued at £2, offensive behaviour and threatening language to Police Inspector Robson." Jack Lang still declared the bridge open that warm Saturday afternoon and it was estimated than one million people walked across it.

Phar Lap was now ready to play his part in the momentous weekend. His race was the 12th on the big program and there was a long delay between it and the previous race. Woodcock asked the reason for it and was told it was a matter of tactics against Phar Lap, whom some suspected could have been given a "go fast" drug. Woodcock was told if Phar Lap's "alarm" was set to go off early the effects would wear off before the start.
Woodcock recalled in his memoirs:

"I couldn't help tell them Phar Lap didn't want any alarm clocks to wake him up, and then I was told that others in the race possibly did."

Happy times in Mexico ... Billy Elliot (left) with Mr David Davis, Tommy Woodcock and vet Bill Nielsen.

In her 1964 biography *"PHAR LAP - the story of the big horse"*, Isabel Carter captures the atmosphere of Agua Caliente:

"Tijuana, cradled between rolling hills leading to distant mountains, was a wide-open town. Prohibition was in full swing in America, and Americans swarmed across the border - particularly at weekends - in a stampede from the rigours of a "dry" United States, with its attendant evils of bootleg liquor and speakeasies. Though Agua Caliente was called a jockey club, horse-racing was only one facet of this playground of gamblers and racketeers. Gambling casinos, poker and roulette saloons, race betting - everything was there to part the visitor from his wad of dollars. Big-time professional gamblers included Caliente in their itinerary, and gangsters, racketeers and bootleggers rubbed shoulders with film stars, politicians and racing men."

Tijuana then, 1932 style, was a product of the lawless prohibition era on one hand, and a warm playground for merrymakers on the other. Pre-race headlines in America such as "Eyes of Turf World Turned Towards (Mexican) Border" resulted in an estimated 20,000 people visiting the town, being a mixture of the rich and famous and racketeers.

Phar Lap made them re-write the headlines the next day, by coming from last position to win in record time of 2:2.8, clipping .2 of a second from the previous track record. An American report added Mr Davis collected US$332,700 from the win: US$50,000 in prizemoney plus a colossal US$282,700 in bets. The Los Angeles "special service" cable which was page one lead story in the March 22 edition of the Sydney *Daily Telegraph* said:

> *"With the dollar at $3.65 to the £1, it is estimated here that Phar Lap's connections here and in Australia won almost £100,000 when Australia's wonder horse took the Agua Caliente Handicap."*

Phar Lap's spectacular win was splashed across papers all over America and Australia. *The Los Angeles Examiner's Chet Koeppel* reported:

> *"Well, the ballyhoo was no dream. A great racehorse, termed the 'Terror of the Antipodes', came 10,000 miles from kangaroo land, made his American debut with a reputation excelled, perhaps, by no thoroughbred, unless you wish to argue Man O'War, and today proved himself a runner that can be regarded as the greatest any Agua Caliente attendance has ever seen. And one that will, or should, if kept in America, be the sensation of the racing for the last decade.....*
>
> *....Phar Lap, the sensation of Australia, startled racing fans by storming from last in the back stretch. By the time they got to the half-mile post the race was over. Phar Lap was a length and a half in front and nothing could touch him. Around the turn into the stretch they thundered. Elliot again had taken a tight hold on his mount. Wholey was riding Reveille Boy like a demon. Only a head in front, the Australian turned into the last quarter (two furlongs). But*

Tommy Woodcock puts a lead strap on Phar Lap, with Billy Elliot atop, after he returns to scale following his win at Agua Caliente.

> *Amid the razzamatazz that followed the win Phar Lap stepped backwards down a terrace of concrete steps, heavily bumping the back of his near fore, and badly bruised the tendon. Years later Woodcock told the author the injury would have put Phar Lap out of training for months and he might never have fully recovered.*

he has champion's blood. No challenge could stop him then, and once only Elliot used the whip. He slashed Phar Lap's flanks and the sturdy Australian leaped, as if fired from a gun. He left Reveille Boy as if the latter was standing still. In a fraction of a second he was two lengths in front..."

Ralph Houston, of *The Los Angeles Times* wrote:

"Phar Lap ran today like the great racehorse he is. Last to leave the barrier, he had to pass every horse in the race to win. He had to thunder by the fleet Cabezo.
He had to withstand the challenge of Reveille Boy. He had to pack topweight of 129 pounds over a mile and a quarter against 10 horses trained to the utmost to beat him. He had to run on a dirt track for the first time in his brilliant career.
He had to break a track record. He had to go to the post without a single preparatory race under his belt. He had to do all of these things to win, but win he did in a manner which left no argument. Phar Lap is not only a fine racehorse, he is one of the greatest which ever lived!"

Amid the razzamatazz that followed the win Phar Lap stepped back just as Hollywood actress Clair Windsor and an Australian woman, Mrs Leon Gordon, were trying to put a garland of flowers around his neck. He stepped backwards down a terrace of concrete steps, heavily bumping the back of his near fore, and badly bruised the tendon as he balanced himself on his hindlegs. Years later Woodcock told the author the injury would have put Phar Lap out of training for months and he might never have fully recovered.

News of the injury was "hushed up" because the Agua Caliente Club wanted Mr Davis to agree to starting the horse the following Sunday in the two miles Agua Caliente Cup. But the chance of him starting was nil.

The injury not being reported in Australia and New Zealand, Phar Lap's triumph outshone everything. Bradman had gone to England and set all manner of batting records in the 1930 Test series and now, 18 months later, Phar Lap had demolished the Americans. In Mexico however, Woodcock was anxious to depart as quickly as possible from the ritzy gambling oasis.

He was also apprehensive about a group led by a man known around the Agua Caliente stabling barn as *"The Brazilian"*. Speaking of this person later, Woodcock wrote:

> *"When Phar Lap won the Agua Caliente Handicap, fulfilling the mission for which he had set out, I was very much relieved. There was a fearful din as he passed the post, and above it all I heard angry words behind me. On looking round I saw the gang, and it was evident someone was telling "The Brazilian" off. The only words I caught were uttered by the little rat who screeched out that Phar Lap had won the race on three legs.*
>
> *We packed our traps a few days later and journeyed to Tanforan, about 600 miles away, and believe me, I was glad to see the end of Mexico."*

Phar Lap was floated to Menlo Park, near Tanforan racecourse on the outskirts of San Francisco, where he rested at the richly appointed farm of Mr Ed Perry, a prominent owner-breeder of gallopers and trotters.

Back in Australia, it was Easter Carnival time at Randwick and Premier Lang was refusing to pay the Federal Government almost £1 million which the NSW Government owed because of the grim financial situation of the Depression. For Phar Lap, Woodcock, trackwork rider Martin and jockey Elliot, it was a time of pure relaxation at the Perry ranch. On Thursday, March 31, a workman sprayed a lead-arsenate poison mixture on some oak trees on the west side of the farm because caterpillars had taken hold.

Woodcock knew something was wrong with Phar Lap on the morning of Tuesday, April 5, exactly two weeks after he had left Agua Caliente. "Big Red" refused his normal sugar cube offering and Woodcock said the horse was listless and a "bit cranky". He called Bill Nielsen who considered Phar Lap was probably suffering from early effects of colic - heavy pain in the abdomen - but by 11 a.m. Phar Lap was in dreadful pain, so much so Nielsen gave him a morphine injection. He knew by this time the trouble was not simply colic. Phar Lap was sweating heavily, the gentle giant was desperately ill and staggering, barely able to stand up. He collapsed on Woodcock, his head bumping the side of the stable door as he went down. Woodcock recalled in his memoirs:

> *"He whinnied. He groaned. Dementedly I rushed around to make him*

Tommy Woodcock ... knew something was wrong with Phar Lap when he refused his normal sugar cube offering and Woodcock said the horse was listless and a "bit cranky".

comfortable. Coming towards me, he nosed affectionately under my arm. Then something inside him burst.

"He drenched me in blood and fell dead at my feet. I will never get over the shock".

Later, ranch owner Perry criticised Woodcock. He said: "The people who handled Phar Lap were responsible for his death. They made two foolish mistakes - letting him eat green alfalfa and feeding him grain brought from Australia, which had become musty and damp. I had told Phar Lap's handlers not to let the horse into a particular alfalfa pasture, but evidently the horse did get in."

Veterinary surgeon, Dr T.R. Creely said: "Phar Lap's stomach and intestines were alive with bot flies - hundreds of them. These parasites, plus bad grain, killed the horse, nothing else. I diagnosed the case as colic, pure and simple."

"Cardigan", who was holidaying at San Francisco, rushed to Menlo Park on hearing from Nielsen that Phar Lap was under treatment. He reported in the *Daily Telegraph* on April 7 that Phar Lap died of an "irritant poison".

"After conducting an autopsy on Phar Lap today, the veterinary surgeon Dr Nielsen declared the horse died from the effects of an irritant poison," "Cardigan" wrote.

"The contents of the stomach have been sent for analysis to California and the result will be known tomorrow. Mr Davis, Phar Lap's part-owner, arrived at Menlo Park late tonight and discussed the cause of death with Nielsen and Woodcock.

"He refused to comment on the horse's death, saying he preferred to wait until the analyst gave his report. He appeared heart-broken, saying continually 'It's terrible. It's terrible'.

"Whether Nielsen's opinion will be borne out by the analyst's report is difficult to say, but Nielsen states emphatically that his experience convinces him it is a case of poisoning.

"Nielsen said tonight: 'I saw the lining of Phar Lap's stomach and I know what it means when the lining is eaten away. I would like to be able to come to some other conclusion, but it is impossible in the face of the evidence of my

Vet Bill Nielsen ... said Phar Lap died from the effects of an irritant poison.

own eyes.'

"Woodcock states the horse was always under lock and key and vigilance was never relaxed for an instant. "Everything the horse ate, he states, was carefully inspected.

"Everything Phar Lap did in America was regarded as big news, but in death he was even more important, as he actually pushed the Lindberg baby case off the front pages." (That case involved the kidnapping of famous pilot Colonel Lindberg's baby in New York.)

An indication of American sentiment was the action by radio station KMTR in Los Angeles, which asked listeners to stand by for 30 seconds as a mark of respect for Phar Lap while a bugler played. Australia, too, was stunned. One Sydney writer commented:

"The thousands who live for the turf and the thousands who can't tell a thoroughbred from a cab hack - all Australia has reason to mourn the swift end that came to a nation's dumb hero, mighty Phar Lap."

"Cardigan" reported on Monday, April 11:

"It now seems certain Phar Lap's death was caused by lead or arsenic poisoning, blown on to the pasture during tree-spraying."

Four years later Woodcock strongly denied Phar Lap's death was caused by carelessness on his part or by the feed. He wrote:

"I knew in my heart that 'Bobby' was poisoned and had a fair idea of the perpetrator, but what was the use?

Menlo Park, where Phar Lap died, was inundated with analysts, inquiry agents, police, photographers and pressmen. I realised that to voice my suspicions would involve me in endless trouble; and nothing could bring my big baby back to me. The analysts engaged by Mr Davis declared there was not sufficient poison found in Phar Lap to kill him, but Government analysts said there was enough arsenate of lead found to bring about his painful end."

Years later he also refuted the theory that Phar Lap had eaten the oak tree leaves which had been sprayed at the Perry farm. "All he ate was good tucker", he told the author.

Phar Lap's hide was stripped from his beautifully moulded frame and an American taxidermist went to work on the magnificent project that now stands so proudly and is gratefully viewed by thousands of people each year at the Melbourne Museum. His huge, fighting heart, was taken to Canberra, where it is also on display.

Harry Telford and Tommy Woodcock were never on friendly terms after Phar Lap's death. Telford suffered lean times as a trainer during most of the 1940's, his last important race success being with Silver Hawk who won the 1953 Rosehill Guineas, which, by coincidence, was the classic which started Phar Lap on his major race winning spree. Telford died at Bacchus Marsh in 1960, aged 83.

David Davis continued to succeed in business as the Depression lifted, spending most of his time raising horses at his home in the USA.

Tommy Woodcock became a successful trainer in his own right in Melbourne, with his best horse being the crack, slow-maturing stayer Reckless, winner of the 1977 Sydney, Adelaide and Brisbane Cups. And, oh, how the crowd was willing him to win the Melbourne Cup of that year, only to see him lose gallantly to Gold And Black. Woodcock died, aged 81, in 1986.

The great Jim Pike failed as a trainer after retiring from the saddle in 1936. He lost a fortune as a punter and then spent his twilight years working as a race day assistant to the very successful Randwick trainer, Jack Green, who had admired his jockey skills.

The Keeper of the Australian Stud Book, Mr John Digby, estimates more than 750,000 thoroughbred foals have been born in New Zealand and Australia since Phar Lap was foaled in 1926.

None was as good. **Big Red** *still stands tall as the exception. He is still the benchmark for champions of the past - and the future.*

PHAR LAP FACT FILE

RACE RECORD: 51 starts; 37 wins, three seconds and two thirds.

STAKEMONEY: £56,425 in Australia + US$50,000 for Agua Caliente

BREEDING: Night Raid - Entreaty (by Winkie)

FOALED: Timaru, New Zealand

DIED: Menlo Park, California, April 5, 1932

OWNERS: Messrs D. J. Davis & H. R. Telford

TRAINER: H. R. Telford

COLOR: Chestnut (near red, hence his nickname "Big Red")

HEIGHT: 17.1 hands

RACING COLORS: *1929-30*

Red jacket, black & white hooped sleeves, red cap

1931-1932

Red jacket, green and red hooped sleeves, black cap

BIGGEST WINS: Agua Caliente Hcp; Melbourne Cup; Victoria & A.J.C. Derbys, W. S. Cox Plate (twice).

THE RECORD

Age	Starts	1st	2nd	3rd	Unpl.	Prizemoney
2	5	1	-	-	4	£182
3	20	13	1	2	4	£26,794
4	16	14	2	-	-	£24,671
5	10	9	-	-	1	£4,778 + US$50,000
TOTAL	51	37	3	2	9	£56,425 +$U.S.50,000 (worth approx. £13,700) for total of £70,125

THE JOCKEYS

Jockey	Rides	Wins	2nds	3rds	Unpl.
J. Pike	30	27	2	-	1
*W. Elliot	7	7	-	-	-
J. Brown	3	-	1	-	2
J. Baker	2	1	-	-	1
R. Lewis	2	-	-	2	-
H. D. Martin	2	-	-	-	2
J. Simpson	2	-	-	-	2
J. Munro	1	1	-	-	-
W. Duncan	1	1	-	-	-
F. Douglas	1	-	-	-	1

* Includes win at Agua Caliente

Billy Elliot ... perfect record in seven rides on Phar Lap

ROSEHILL

Saturday, April 27, 1929

MAIDEN JUVENILE HCP

(Two-year-olds)
6 furlongs

1	**Phar Lap**			
	7.9	....	J. Baker	£182
2	**Voleuse**			
	7.6	....	W. Cook	£40
3	**Pure Tea**			
	8.12	....	M. McCarten	£20

WON BY
½ len, 2 len. Time: 1:15½

ALSO RAN

Credit Note	8.12
Red Dust	8.8
King Caravel	8.1
Marie's Pride	8.8
Coucal	8.3
Doubloon	7.7
Polacre	8.0
Provena	7.12
Wolram	7.12
Charmeta	7.10
Roseflight	7.9
Winfield	7.6
Prince Tercian	7.10
Bubalan	7.7
Magster	7.7
Suggestive	7.7
Delle Rose	7.1
Bunyarra	6.10

BETTING

5/2 Pure Tea, 4 Voleuse, 6 Roseflight, 7 Phar Lap, 8 Credit Note

MAIDEN JUVENILE HANDICAP, *(Rosehill, 27/4/1929)*

Phar Lap 1st *(7.9 J. Baker) ....* ***Voleuse 2nd .... Pure Tea 3rd*** *.... Won by: ½ len .... Time: 1:15½*

ROSEHILL

Saturday, September 21, 1929

ROSEHILL GUINEAS

(Three-year-olds)
9 furlongs

1	*Phar Lap*		
	8.5 .... J. Munro		£913
2	*Lorason*		
	8.5 .... R. Reed		£210
3	*Holdfast*		
	8.5 .... M. McCarten		£105

WON BY
3 len, 2½ len. Time: 1:52 (Equal race record)

ALSO RAN

Peacemaker	8.5
Wooodgera	8.5
Toper	8.5
Parkwood	8.5
Phantom Reef	8.5
Pentheus	8.5
Magnifier	8.5
King Crow	8.5
Firbolg	8.5

BETTING

2 Phar Lap, 4 Parkwood, 5 Toper, 6 Pentheus, 7 Holdfast, 8 Lorason

ROSEHILL GUINEAS, *(Rosehill, 21/9/1929)*

Phar Lap 1st (8.5 J. Munro) .... **Lorason 2nd** .... **Holdfast 3rd** .... Won by: 3 len .... Time: 1:52 (Equal race record)

RANDWICK

Saturday, October 5, 1929

A.J.C. DERBY

(Three-year-olds)
1½ miles

1	**Phar Lap**			
	8.10	.... J. Pike		£7,135
2	**Carradale**			
	8.10	.... A. Wilson		£1,600
3	**Honour**			
	8.10	.... T. Green		£800

WON BY
3½ len, 8 len. Time: 2:31¼ (Race record)

ALSO RAN

Comanche	8.10	M. McCarten	4
Lorason	8.10	J. Munro	5
Sir Ribble	8.10	J. Crowley	6
Pentheus	8.10	R. Reed	7
Nedda	8.5	J. Cook	8
Cathmar	8.10	E. Bartle	0
Toper	8.10	W. Cook	0
Queen Nassau	8.5	W. Johnstone	0

BETTING

5/4 Phar Lap, 9/2 Carradale, Comanche, Honour, 20 Toper, Pentheus, 25 Lorason, 33 Cathmar, Sir Ribble, Nedda, 50 Queen Nassau

A.J.C. DERBY, (Randwick, 5/10/1929)

Phar Lap 1st (8.10 J. Pike) .... **Carradale 2nd** .... **Honour 3rd** .... Won by: 3½ len .... Time: 2:31¼ (Race record)

RANDWICK

Wednesday, October 9, 1929

CRAVEN PLATE

(Weight-for-Age)
10 furlongs

1	*Phar Lap* 7.8	W. Duncan	£2,205
2	*Mollison* 8.11	W. Cook	£600
3	*Amounis* 9.1	J. Munro	£300

WON BY
4 len, 10 len. Time: 2:11¼

ALSO RAN

Loquacious 8.9 M. McCarten 0

BETTING

5/4 Phar Lap, Mollison, 7 Loquacious, 14 Amounis

CRAVEN PLATE, *(Randwick, 9/10/1929)*

Phar Lap 1st (7.8 W. Duncan) .... **Mollison 2nd** .... **Amounis 3rd** .... *Won by: 4 len .... Time: 2:11¼*

FLEMINGTON

Saturday, November 2, 1929

VICTORIA DERBY

(Three-year-olds)
1½ miles

1   *Phar Lap*
         8.10 .... J. Pike   £4,456
2   *Carradale*
         8.10 .... A. Wilson   £1,000
3   *Taisho*
         8.10 .... J. Munro   £500

WON BY
2 len, ½ len. Time: 2:31¼ (Race record)

ALSO RAN

Limber Up	8.10	*W. Duncan*	4
Third King	8.10	*R. Lewis*	5
Temoin	8.10	*W. Elliot*	6
Pentheus	8.10	*M. McCarten*	7

BETTING

2/9 Phar Lap, 10 Carradale, 12 Pentheus, 15 Taisho, 33 Limber Up, 100 Temoin, Third King

VICTORIA DERBY, *(Flemington, 2/11/1929)*

Phar Lap 1st *(8.10 J. Pike)* .... **Carradale 2nd** .... **Taisho 3rd** .... *Won by: 2 len .... Time: 2:31¼ (Race record)*

FLEMINGTON

Saturday, March 1, 1930

ST. LEGER STAKES

(Three-year-olds)
14 furlongs

1	**Phar Lap**		
	8.10 .... J. Pike		£1,691
2	**Sir Ribble**		
	8.10 .... W. Johnstone		£300
3	**Lineage**		
	8.7 .... F. Dempsey		£150

WON BY
5 len, 2 len. Time: 3:1¼ (Equal Race record)

ALSO RAN

Romany Rye	8.10	N. Percival	4
Cragford	8.10	R. Lewis	0

BETTING

1/2 Phar Lap, 4 Sir Ribble, 5 Lineage, 12 Romany Rye, 15 Cragford

ST. LEGER STAKES, *(Flemington, 1/3/1930)*

Phar Lap 1st *(8.10 J. Pike)* .... **Sir Ribble 2nd** .... **Lineage 3rd** .... *Won by: 5 len* .... *Time: 3:1¼ (Equal race record)*

FLEMINGTON

Thursday, March 6, 1930

GOVERNOR'S PLATE

(Weight-for-Age)
1½ miles

1	*Phar Lap*		
	7.13 .... W. Elliot		£749
2	*Lineage*		
	7.13 .... F. Dempsey		£200
3	*High Syce*		
	9.3 .... A. Reed		£100

WON BY
4 len, 4 len. Time: 2:30¼

ALSO RAN
Jeypore   9.0   W. Cook   0

BETTING

4/9 Phar Lap, 5/2 High Syce, 33 Jeypore, Lineage

GOVERNOR'S PLATE, *(Flemington, 6/3/1930)*

Phar Lap 1st *(7.13 W. Elliot)* .... **Lineage 2nd** .... **High Syce 3rd** .... *Won by: 4 len* .... *Time: 2:30¼*

FLEMINGTON

Saturday, March 8, 1930

KING'S PLATE

(Weight-for-Age)
2 miles

1	*Phar Lap*		
	7.11 .... W. Elliot		£1,112
2	*Second Wind*		
	8.11 .... A. Wilson		£300
3	*Lineage*		
	7.11 .... F. Dempsey		£150

WON BY
20 len, 3 len. Time: 3:25

ALSO RAN

Mondiaga	9.1	H. Jones	4
Some Quality	9.1	N. Percival	0

BETTING

1/10 Phar Lap, 15 Lineage, 20 Second Wind, 33 Mondiaga, Some Quality

KING'S PLATE, *(Flemington, 8/3/1930)*

Phar Lap 1st *(7.11 W. Elliot) .... ***Second Wind 2nd**** .... Lineage 3rd .... Won by: 20 len .... Time: 3:25*

WARWICK FARM

Saturday, April 12, 1930

CHIPPING NORTON STAKES

(Weight-for-Age)
10 furlongs

1	***Phar Lap***	
	8.10 .... J. Pike	£747
2	***Amounis***	
	9.6 .... H. Jones	£200
3	***Nightmarch***	
	9.7 .... R. Reed	£100

WON BY
2 len, neck. Time: 2:6

ALSO RAN

Donald   8.13
Cathmar   8.9

BETTING

5/4 Phar Lap, 2 Amounis, 5/2 Nightmarch, 100 Cathmar, Donald

CHIPPING NORTON STAKES, (Warwick Farm, 12/4/1930)

Phar Lap 1st *(8.10 J. Pike) .... **Amounis 2nd** .... **Nightmarch 3rd** .... Won by: 2 len .... Time: 2:6*

RANDWICK

Saturday, April 19, 1930

A.J.C. ST. LEGER

(Three-year-olds)
14 furlongs

1	*Phar Lap*	
	8.10 .... J. Pike	£2,478
2	*Sir Ribble*	
	8.10 .... W. Johnstone	£500
3	*Peacemaker*	
	8.10 .... A. Wilson	£250

WON BY
3½ len, 1½ len. Time: 3:7

BETTING

1/20 Phar Lap, 20 Peacemaker, Sir Ribble

A.J.C. ST. LEGER, *(Randwick, 19/4/1930)*

Phar Lap 1st *(8.10 J. Pike)* .... **Sir Ribble 2nd** .... **Peacemaker 3rd** .... *Won by: 3½ len* .... *Time: 3:7*

RANDWICK

Wednesday, April 23, 1930

CUMBERLAND STAKES

(Weight-for-Age)
14 furlongs

1	*Phar Lap*		
	8.1 .... W. Elliot		£1,457
2	*Donald*		
	9.0 .... S. Davidson		£400
3	*Kidaides*		
	9.0 .... N. Percival		£200

WON BY
2 len, 20 len. Time: 2:58¾

NO BETTING

CUMBERLAND STAKES, *(Randwick, 23/4/1930)*

Phar Lap 1st *(8.1 W. Elliot)* .... **Donald 2nd** .... **Kidaides 3rd** .... *Won by: 2 len .... Time: 2:58¾*

RANDWICK

Saturday, April 26, 1930

A.J.C. PLATE

(Weight-for-Age)
2¼ miles

1	*Phar Lap*		
	7.13 .... W. Elliot		£1,451
2	*Nightmarch*		
	9.0 .... R. Reed		£400
3	*Donald*		
	9.1 .... S. Davidson		£200

WON BY
10 len, ¾ len. Time: 3:49½ (Australasian record)

BETTING

2/5 Phar Lap, 9/4 Nightmarch, 33 Donald

A.J.C. PLATE, (Randwick, 26/4/1930)

Phar Lap 1st (7.13 W. Elliot) .... **Nightmarch 2nd** .... Donald 3rd .... Won by: 10 len .... Time: 3:49½ (Australasian record)

MORPHETTVILLE

Saturday, May 10, 1930

ELDER STAKES

(Weight-for-Age)
9 furlongs

1	***Phar Lap***	
	8.4 .... W. Elliot	£325
2	***Fruition***	
	8.13 .... E. Whittaker	£50

WON BY
5 len. Time: 1:52

NO BETTING

ELDER STAKES, *(Morphettville, 10/5/1930)*

Phar Lap 1st *(8.4 W. Elliot)* .... **Fruition 2nd** .... *Won by: 5 len .... Time: 1:52*

MORPHETTVILLE

Saturday, May 17, 1930

KING'S CUP

1½ miles

1	*Phar Lap*			
		9.5 .... J. Pike		£800
2 *	*Nadean*			
		8.2 .... L. Miller		£150
2 *	*Kirrkie*			
		7.10 .... N. Percival		£150

WON BY

3½ len, dead-heat. Time: 2:34

ALSO RAN

Temptation	7.0	R. Evans	4
Mary Spa	7.6	G. Mules	5
Kidaides	8.7	T. Spain	0

NO BETTING

KING'S CUP, (Morphettville, 17/5/1930)

Phar Lap 1st (9.5 J. Pike) .... **Nadean =2nd** .... **Kirrkie =2nd** .... Won by: 3½ len .... Time: 2:34

RANDWICK

Saturday, September 13, 1930

CHELMSFORD STAKES

(Weight-for-Age)
9 furlongs

1	*Phar Lap*			
		9.4	*J. Pike*	£1,033
2	*Nightmarch*			
		9.11	*R. Reed*	£200
3	*Weotara*			
		7.6	*J. Simpson*	£100

WON BY
2½ len, short neck. Time: 1:51½

ALSO RAN

Concentrate	9.8
Loquacious	9.6
Burracootboo	7.9
Income	7.6

BETTING

1/5 Phar Lap, 9/2 Nightmarch, 33 Loquacious, 100 Weotara

CHELMSFORD STAKES, *(Randwick, 13/9/1930)*

Phar Lap 1st *(9.4 J. Pike)* .... **Nightmarch 2nd** .... **Weotara 3rd** .... *Won by: 2½ len .... Time: 1:51½*

ROSEHILL

Saturday, September 20, 1930

HILL STAKES

(Weight-for-Age)
1 mile

1	*Phar Lap*		
	9.4 .... J. Pike		£597
2	*Nightmarch*		
	9.3 .... R. Reed		£150
3	*High Disdain*		
	9.0 .... W. Cook		£75

WON BY

Len, 1½ len. Time: 1:40

ALSO RAN

Don Moon	9.0
Limerick	9.0
Concentrate	9.0
Western Lass	8.12

BETTING

2/7 Phar Lap, 4 Nightmarch, 33 High Disdain

HILL STAKES, (Rosehill, 20/9/1930)

Phar Lap 1st (9.4 J. Pike) .... **Nightmarch 2nd** .... **High Disdain 3rd** .... Won by: 1 len .... Time: 1:40

RANDWICK

Saturday, October 4, 1930

SPRING STAKES

(Weight-for-Age)
1½ miles

1	*Phar Lap*		
	8.11 .... J. Pike		£1,467
2	*Nightmarch*		
	9.5 .... R. Reed		£400
3	*Concentrate*		
	9.2 .... A. Reed		£200

WON BY
½ len, 8 len. Time: 2:33¼

ALSO RAN

Dalston	9.0	E. Bartle	4
Tressilian	9.3	M. McCarten	0

BETTING

1/10 Phar Lap, 7 Nightmarch, 33 Concentrate

SPRING STAKES, *(Randwick, 4/10/1930)*

Phar Lap 1st *(8.11 J. Pike)* .... **Nightmarch 2nd** .... **Concentrate 3rd** .... *Won by: ½ len .... Time: 2:33¼*

RANDWICK

Wednesday, October 8, 1930

CRAVEN PLATE

(Weight-for-Age)
10 furlongs

1	*Phar Lap*	8.11	J. Pike	£1,830
2	*Nightmarch*	9.4	R. Reed	£500
3	*Donald*	9.2	S. Davidson	£250

WON BY
6 len, 10 len. Time: 2:3 (Australasian Record)

ALSO RAN:
Limerick   9.1   M. McCarten   0

BETTING
1/6 Phar Lap, 5 Nightmarch, 20 Limerick, Donald

CRAVEN PLATE, *(Randwick, 8/10/1930)*

Phar Lap 1st *(8.11 J. Pike)* .... **Nightmarch 2nd** .... **Donald 3rd** .... Won by: 6 len .... Time: 2:3 *(Australasian record)*

RANDWICK

Saturday, October 11, 1930

RANDWICK PLATE

(Weight-for-Age)
2 miles

1	*Phar Lap*		
	8.11 .... J. Pike		£1,465
2	*Donald*		
	9.4 .... S. Davidson		£400
3	*Concentrate*		
	9.3 .... M. McCarten		£200

WON BY
2 len, 3 len. Time: 3:36¼

NO BETTING

RANDWICK PLATE, *(Randwick, 11/10/1930)*

Phar Lap 1st *(8.11 J. Pike)* .... **Donald 2nd** .... **Concentrate 3rd** .... *Won by: 2 len .... Time: 3:36¼*

MOONEE VALLEY

Saturday, October 25, 1930

W. S. COX PLATE

(Weight-for-Age)
9½ furlongs

1	*Phar Lap*			
	8.11	.... J. Pike		£850
2	*Tregilla*			
	7.11	.... E. Bartle		£150
3	*Mollison*			
	9.1	.... J. Daniels		£100

WON BY

4 len, 1 len. Time: 1:59¼

ALSO RAN

Veilmond	7.11	W. Cook	4
Donald	9.1	S. Davidson	5
Fulham	7.8	W. Duncan	0

BETTING

1/7 Phar Lap, 10 Tregilla, Mollison, Veilmond, 50 Donald, Fulham

W. S. COX PLATE, *(Moonee Valley, 25/10/1930)*

Phar Lap 1st *(8.11 J. Pike)* .... **Tregilla 2nd** .... **Mollison 3rd** .... *Won by: 4 len .... Time: 1:59¼*

FLEMINGTON

Saturday, November 1, 1930

MELBOURNE STAKES

(Weight-for-Age)
10 furlongs

1	*Phar Lap*		
	8.11 .... J. Pike		£1,000
2	*Tregilla*		
	7.12 .... E. Bartle		£200
3	*Amounis*		
	9.0 .... W. Cook		£100

WON BY
3 len, 4 len. Time: 2:4½

ALSO RAN

| Carradale | 9.0 | H. Jones | 4 |
| Donald | 9.0 | S. Davidson | 0 |

BETTING

1/5 Phar Lap, 6 Amounis, 16 Tregilla, 25 Carradale, 100 Donald

MELBOURNE STAKES, *(Flemington, 1/11/1930)*

Phar Lap 1st (8.11 J. Pike) .... **Tregilla 2nd** .... **Amounis 3rd** .... Won by: 3 len .... Time: 2:4½

HOW PHAR LAP WON THE CUP

Melbourne *Herald* report on Phar Lap's Win

Striding away from the pacemaker, Temptation, at the top of the straight, Phar Lap drew right away to win the Melbourne Cup this afternoon with ridiculous ease from Second Wind and Shadow King.

When the assembled thousands realised that Phar Lap had the race won, and Tregilla had failed in his run to overhaul the champion, Flemington "went mad". Phar Lap ran over the last furlong with consummate ease, and no Melbourne Cup would have been won in more stylish or more effortless manner.

It was the crowning triumph of Phar Lap's remarkable career, and, where he failed to win the Melbourne Cup last year, he more than atoned for that defeat by his peerless performance this afternoon. Phar Lap's Cup will always be remembered as one of the most sensational, as on Saturday an attempt was made to shoot him. After that occurrence he was spirited away from Melbourne for the few remaining days before the Cup, and these he spent in peaceful seclusion at St. Albans, some miles beyond Geelong.

Career of Records

Phar Lap has been breaking records throughout his rather brief turf career, as he did today, with 12lb. more under the weight-for-age scales, what Carbine failed to achieve as a four-year-old in 1889.

Phar Lap created a further record today- at 11/8 on, he ranks as the hottest favorite to win the Melbourne Cup. He started at even money last year when he was beaten, but there was seldom better than even money bet today. Long before the race was run, he was at odds-on all over the paddock ring.

Some time before the first race was run, a leading Melbourne bookmaker laid £5000 to £4000 against Phar Lap. Tregilla was always hovering between 4/1 and 5/1, and Balloon King, who was next in demand, was always at a double figure quotation. Outside of these three horses there was not a great deal of support for any of the other runners. Some of the principal wagers on the Cup were: £4500 to £1000 Tregilla; £3000 to £150, £2000 to £80, and $1000 to £50 (twice) Carradale; £500 to £16/10/- and £500 to £17/10/- (three times) Nadean; £3000 to £150 Veilmond. Another bookmaker laid an even £300 against Phar Lap, and another wager in favor of the champion was £1000 to £800.

John Buchan, who was injured while working at Flemington this morning, was withdrawn on the course, and another Cup scratching was Wapilly. This left 15 to contest the race - one more than when Nightmarch scored a year ago. Phar Lap was not brought to Flemington until some minutes after 2 p.m., and he was carefully guarded by the police right up to the time he had to go to the post. Phar Lap, who looked in wonderful condition, led the parade of the Cup runners on to the course proper, and on his way down the lane he was given a wonderful reception.

The only incident as the horses were going to the post was when Shadow King broke away from the line as he reached the track, and he galloped down the straight to the starting post, where he arrived several minutes before any other candidate.

Phar Lap was given a steady preliminary but Pike had to restrain him, as he was eager to go fast. No horse could have looked fitter for the herculean task that confronted him. Phar Lap was accompanied to the post by one of the clerks of the course. There was very little delay at the barrier, and one minute after the scheduled time of starting, the field was off on its long journey. One of the first to break the line was the light weight Temptation, and Pike pulled Phar Lap into about fourth place before the field had gone a furlong.

Temptation Still Ahead

Coming to the junction of the courses, Temptation had taken charge. Running down the straight to the judge's box for the first time, Temptation, who was setting a fairly fast pace, was slightly in front of Carradale. Just behind them was First Acre on the rails. Phar Lap was about half a length on the outside of First Acre, while Shadow King, Nadean and Star God were all prominent. Veilmond, who began slowly, was a clear last as the field swung out of the straight, where Temptation had drawn away from Carradale. First Acre and Phar Lap were following.

Phar Lap was travelling very easily, and Pike seemed to be having no trouble in guiding him behind his field. As the field left the straight, Tregilla was fourth last, and only Some Quality and Veilmond were behind him.

Running along the river side, Temptation, who was pulling hard, had opened up a gap of four lengths from Carradale, Phar Lap, Muratti, Star God and First Acre, while Tregilla had not improved his position. Balloon King was also a long way back. The pace set by Temptation appeared to suit Phar Lap admirably, as he was soon holding his position - about fourth place - without any apparent effort. A little further on Muratti began to drop back. Tregilla, by the time the seven was reached, was still near the tail of the field, and Veilmond so far had not passed a horse in the race.

Seven furlongs from home, Temptation was still four or five lengths in front of Carradale. Star God had improved his position rather quickly and had run into first place. First Acre was just behind him, in company with Phar Lap. Soulton made a forward move at this point, and so did Some Quality, and they were not far behind the favorite. Tregilla, who had worked his way up on the outside, was running next. Coming to the home turn, Temptation still maintained his advantage, and at this point Pike took Phar Lap on to the rails. Tregilla moved up on the outside.

As the field turned into the straight, Pike let Phar Lap have his head, and in a few strides the Melbourne Cup of 1930 was all over. Tregilla made a dash at him about two furlongs from home, but his effort was short-lived, and he quickly began to tire. Phar Lap began gradually to open up a gap between him and his pursuers, and more than a furlong from home he had a lead of three lengths. Pike was letting him run along on his own.

Pike did not have to move on Phar Lap, who won with his ears pricked. It was palpable, from the determined and comfortable manner in which he finished, that he could have gone much further. When Tregilla began to drop back in the straight, Second Wind, Shadow King, Donald and First Acre began an interesting struggle for second position. Second Wind, who finished much better than was generally expected, gained that honor. Third place went to Shadow King, who hung on exceptionally well, and he was only the merest fraction in front of Donald.

None of the beaten horses finished faster than Veilmond, and he was finishing gamely when the post was reached. Veilmond made a great run from the half-mile, where he was still last. Soulton, who was going well half a mile from home, did not run out the distance. One of the surprises of the race was the performance of the New Zealander, First Acre, who finished close to the placed horses.

<u>Triumph for Pike</u>

Old Donald was another who finished well. Carradale, after running a fair race for a large portion of the journey, was last home. The two South Australians, Nadean and Some Quality, were never dangerous, and Balloon King did not display the stamina that was generally expected of him. Star God was one of the leaders half a mile from the post, but he too failed to run out the two miles. Muratti was beaten a long way from home.

Temptation admirably filled the role of pacemaker, and he ran well until the last two furlongs, where he found that it was beyond him. He did not improve his prospects by hanging out practically throughout the race. Veilmond might have finished much closer if his rider, W. Cook, had not been struck in an eye by a piece of flying mud. The colt also met with some interference. Balloon King struck some trouble as the field ran along the river side, and after that did not appear to run at all kindly.

Phar Lap is unquestionably one of the greatest racehorses Australia has seen. It was a remarkable performance for the four-year-old to win the Cup so easily with 12lb. over weight-for-age. It was a further triumph for the riding ability of J. Pike, who today was having his 14th ride in a Melbourne Cup. This was his first success.

By winning the Cup today, Phar Lap won £9229 (plus a £200 Gold Cup) and this makes his stake winnings £44,637. Indicating what a phenomenal galloper he is, he has won practically all of that money in about 18 months. Phar Lap is now £2000 or £3000 behind Amounis's Australasian stakes winning record, and if he continues to race as well as he did today, he should have no difficulty in creating a new record.

Never in the history of the race has one horse for so long dominated the Cup position, and his victory will be an exceptionally costly one to the bookmakers. The double, Amounis-Phar Lap, was extensively supported for some months, and it is estimated that in Melbourne alone the ring will have to pay out more than £100,000.

Money was poured on Phar Lap today, and a lot of it was for bookmakers who were attempting to balance their double ledgers. In most cases they had to lay odds on. One of the biggest winners over the double is said to be Sydney's spectacular woman punter.

The intermediate times were: First half mile, 55 sec.; second half mile, 51½; the next half mile, 52½; the last half mile, 49; the last six furlongs, 1:16; and the last mile, 1:41¼. The time for the Cup, 3:27¾ was well outside the record for the race, but the rain which had fallen earlier in the day and a headwind against which the horses had to finish would not make for fast time today.- **GWYN JONES**

Winning important races is part of a day's work for Jim Pike (above), but no more pleased man was at Flemington today than Pike after he had passed the post on Phar Lap.

As is usual with him, he passed most of the credit on to his mount.

"He is a wonderful horse," Pike said. "I was able to let him run along in fourth or fifth place to the turn, and when the opportunity came, I gave him his head and he won like the champion he is.

"He had a good run and the result was never in doubt. Phar Lap is able to do anything you ask of him. When I gave him his head he went away from the field and I think had he been called upon for an extra finishing effort, he would have been well able to respond."

FLEMINGTON

Tuesday, November 4, 1930

MELBOURNE CUP

2 miles

1	*Phar Lap*		
	9.12 .... J. Pike		£9,429
2	*Second Wind*		
	8.12 .... T. Lewis		£2,000
3	*Shadow King*		
	8.4 .... P. Tehan		£1,000

WON BY
3 len, ¾ len. Time: 3:27¾

ALSO RAN

Donald	8.12	S. Davidson	4
Veilmond	7.7	W. Cook	5
First Acre	7.11	T. Webster	6
Tregilla	7.9	E. Bartle	7
Soulton	8.2	F. Dempsey	8
Some Quality	7.11	N. Percival	9
Balloon King	7.6	F. Hickey	0
Carradale	8.9	H. Jones	0
Nadean	8.0	A. Wilson	0
Star God	7.11	W. Johnstone	0
Muratti	7.6	W. Duncan	0
Temptation	7.0	R. Medhurst	0

BETTING

8/11 Phar Lap, 5 Tregilla, 16 Balloon King, 20 Soulton, Nadean, 25 Carradale, Veilmond, Muratti, 40 Star God, 50 Second Wind, Shadow King, Some Quality, Temptation, 66 Donald, 100 First Acre

MELBOURNE CUP, *(Flemington, 4/11/1930)*

Phar Lap 1st *(9.12 J. Pike)* .... **Second Wind 2nd** .... **Shadow King 3rd** .... *Won by: 3 len .... Time: 3:27¾*

FLEMINGTON

Thursday, November 6, 1930

LINLITHGOW STAKES

(Weight-for-Age)
1 mile

1 *Phar Lap*
      8.12 .... J. Pike   £1,000
2 *Mollison*
      8.13 .... J. Daniels   £200
3 *Mystic Peak*
      9.2 .... A. Reed   £100

WON BY
4 len, neck. Time: 1:37

ALSO RAN

| Wise Force | 9.0 | F. Dempsey | 4 |
| Amounis | 8.13 | W. Cook | 0 |

BETTING

1/7 Phar Lap, 12 Amounis, 33 Mystic Peak, Wise Force, Mollison

LINLITHGOW STAKES, *(Flemington, 6/11/1930)*

Phar Lap 1st (8.12 J. Pike) .... **Mollison 2nd** .... **Mystic Peak 3rd** .... Won by: 4 len .... Time: 1:37

FLEMINGTON

Saturday, November 8, 1930

C. B. FISHER PLATE

(Weight-for-Age)
1½ miles

1	*Phar Lap*		
	8.12 .... J. Pike		£1,000
2	*Second Wind*		
	9.1 .... T. Lewis		£200
3	*Lineage*		
	8.9 .... V. Sleigh		£100

WON BY
3½ len, 4 len. Time: 2:48¼

NO BETTING

C. B. FISHER PLATE, *(Flemington, 8/11/1930)*

Phar Lap 1st *(8.12 J. Pike) .... **Second Wind 2nd** .... **Lineage 3rd** .... Won by: 3½ len .... Time: 2:48¼*

CAULFIELD

Saturday, February 14, 1931

ST. GEORGE STAKES

(Weight-for-Age)
9 furlongs

1	*Phar Lap*		
	9.7 .... J. Pike		£600
2	*Induna*		
	8.3 .... F. Dempsey		£100
3	*Glare*		
	8.13 .... G. Truskett		£50

WON BY
2½ len, 2½ len. Time: 1:54¾

ALSO RAN

Black Duchess   9.9   A. Reed   4

BETTING

1/14 Phar Lap

ST GEORGE STAKES, *(Caulfield, 14/2/1931)*

Phar Lap 1st (9.7 J. Pike) .... **Induna 2nd** .... **Glare 3rd** .... Won by: 2½ len .... Time: 1:54¾

CAULFIELD

Saturday, February 21, 1931

FUTURITY STAKES

(Weight-for-Age)
7 furlongs

1	*Phar Lap*			
	10.3	....	J. Pike	£2,600
2	*Mystic Peak*			
	10.2	....	A. Reed	£600
3	*Taurus*			
	8.12	....	C. Selby	£300

WON BY
Neck, len. Time: 1:27¼

ALSO RAN

Mollison	9.8	K. Bracken	4
Greenline	9.8	J. Munro	5
Waterline	8.11	W. Duncan	6
Wise Force	9.12	R. Lewis	7
The Doctor's Orders	8.12	T. Lewis	8
Brazenface	8.12	D. Munro	0
Lightstead	8.2	H. Badger	0

BETTING

1/2 Phar Lap, 4 Waterline, 12 Greenline, 33 Mystic Peak, Mollison, 100 Taurus

FUTURITY STAKES, *(Caulfield, 21/2/1931)*

Phar Lap 1st (10.3 *J. Pike*) .... **Mystic Peak 2nd** .... **Taurus 3rd** .... *Won by: Neck* .... *Time: 1:27¼*

FLEMINGTON

Saturday, February 28, 1931

ESSENDON STAKES

(Weight-for-Age)
10 furlongs

1	*Phar Lap*		
	8.7 .... J. Pike		£700
2	*Lampra*		
	8.0 .... R. Wilson		£200
3	*Mira Donna*		
	7.7 .... H. Morris		£100

WON BY
3 len, 4 len. Time: 2:5½

ALSO RAN

Glare   8.2   F. Dempsey   0

NO BETTING

ESSENDON STAKES, *(Flemington, 28/2/1931)*

Phar Lap 1st (8.7 J. Pike) .... **Lampra 2nd** .... **Mira Donna 3rd** .... Won by: 3 len .... Time: 2:5½

FLEMINGTON

Wednesday, March 4, 1931

THE KING'S PLATE

(Weight-for-Age)
1½ miles

1	*Phar Lap*			
		9.7 .... *J. Pike*		£700
2	*Glare*			
		8.3 .... *F. Dempsey*		£200
3	*Lampra*			
		8.0 .... *R. Wilson*		£100

WON BY
1¼ len, 1½ len. Time: 2:37¼

ALSO RAN

El Ray	8.3	*W. Duncan*	4
Prince Don	8.3	*E. J. Morris*	0

NO BETTING

THE KING'S PLATE, *(Flemington, 4/3/1931)*

Phar Lap 1st *(9.7 J. Pike)* .... ***Glare 2nd*** .... ***Lampra 3rd*** .... *Won by: 1¼ len* .... *Time: 2:37¼*

WILLIAMSTOWN

Tuesday, August 25, 1931

UNDERWOOD STAKES

(Weight-for-Age)
1 mile

1	*Phar Lap*		
	9.0 .... W. Elliot		£350
2	*Rondalina*		
	7.6 .... P. Reynolds		£100
3	*Wise Force*		
	9.3 .... W. Duncan		£50

WON BY
1¾ len, neck. Time: 1:42½

ALSO RAN

Waterline   9.0
Glare   9.0
Mulcra   7.11

BETTING

2/1 Phar Lap, 9/4 Wise Force, Waterline, 33 Rondalina

UNDERWOOD STAKES, *(Williamstown, 25/8/1931)*

Phar Lap 1st *(9.0 W. Elliot)* .... **Rondalina 2nd** .... **Wise Force 3rd** .... *Won by: 1¾ len* .... *Time: 1:42½*

CAULFIELD

Saturday, September 5, 1931

MEMSIE STAKES

(Weight-for-Age)
9 furlongs

1	*Phar Lap*		
	9.8 .... J. Pike		£500
2	*Rondalina*		
	6.11 .... N. Percival		£200
3	*Waterline*		
	9.8 .... W. Scanlon		£100

WON BY
3½ len, hd. Time: 1:52¾

ALSO RAN

Wise Force	9.11	E. J. Morris	4
Glare	9.1	G. Truskett	5
Semitist	7.4	A. Dewhurst	0

BETTING

1/6 Phar Lap, 15 Waterline, 20 Rondalina

MEMSIE STAKES, *(Caulfield, 5/9/1931)*

Phar Lap 1st (9.8 J. Pike) .... **Rondalina 2nd** .... Waterline 3rd .... Won by: 3½ len .... Time: 1:52¾

ROSEHILL

Saturday, September 19, 1931

HILL STAKES

(Weight-for-Age)
1 mile

1	*Phar Lap* 9.0 .... J. Pike	£444
2	*Chide* 9.0 .... M. McCarten	£120
3	*Waugoola* 9.0 .... W. Cook	£60

WON BY
1½ len, 3 len. Time: 1:39½

ALSO RAN
Sir Chrystopher   9.0

NO BETTING

HILL STAKES, *(Rosehill, 19/9/1931)*

Phar Lap 1st *(9.0 J. Pike) .... **Chide 2nd** .... Waugoola 3rd .... Won by: 1½ len .... Time: 1:39½*

RANDWICK

Saturday, October 3, 1931

SPRING STAKES

(Weight-for-Age)
1½ miles

1	**Phar Lap**		
	9.2 .... J. Pike		£779
2	**Chide**		
	9.3 .... W. Cook		£200
3	**The Dimmer**		
	9.3 .... E. Bartle		£100

WON BY
1¼ len, 3 len. Time: 2:33¾

ALSO RAN

Concentrate	9.3	B. Morris	4
First Acre	9.3	T. Webster	5
Loquacious	9.1	J. Munro	0
Carry On	8.9	J. Pratt	0

NO BETTING

SPRING STAKES, *(Randwick, 3/10/1931)*

Phar Lap 1st (9.2 *J. Pike*) .... **Chide 2nd** .... *The Dimmer 3rd* .... *Won by:* 1¼ len .... *Time:* 2:33¾

RANDWICK

Wednesday, October 7, 1931

CRAVEN PLATE

(Weight-for-Age)
10 furlongs

1	*Phar Lap*	9.1	J. Pike	£940
2	*Pentheus*	9.4	J. Munro	£250
3	*Chide*	9.1	W. Cook	£125

WON BY

4 len, 3½ len. Time: 2:2½ (Australasian record)

ALSO RAN

Carry On 8.9 M. McCarten 0

NO BETTING

CRAVEN PLATE, *(Randwick, 7/10/1931)*

Phar Lap 1st *(9.1 J. Pike)* .... ***Pentheus 2nd*** .... ***Chide 3rd*** .... Won by: 4 len .... Time: 2:2½ *(Australasian record)*

RANDWICK

Saturday, October 10, 1931

RANDWICK PLATE

(Weight-for-Age)
2 miles

1	*Phar Lap*		
	9.3 .... J. Pike		$740
2	*Chide*		
	9.4 .... W. Cook		£200

WON BY
4 len. Time: 3:31

NO BETTING

RANDWICK PLATE, *(Randwick, 10/10/1931)*

Phar Lap 1st (9.3 J. Pike) .... **Chide 2nd** .... Won by: 4 len .... Time: 3:31

MOONEE VALLEY

Saturday, October 24, 1931

W. S. COX PLATE

(Weight-for-Age)
9½ furlongs

1	*Phar Lap*		
	9.4 .... J. Pike		£500
2	*Chatham*		
	7.11 .... H. Morris		£150
3	*Johnnie Jason*		
	7.11 .... J. Pratt		£100

WON BY
2½ len, 2 len. Time: 2:1½

ALSO RAN

Le Region	7.11	J. Simpson	4
Veilmond	9.0	J. Munro	5
Carry On	8.9	M. McCarten	6
Cimbrian	9.4	O. Phillips	0

BETTING

1/14 Phar Lap, 6/4 Veilmond, 7/2 Chatham, Johnnie Jason, Cimbrian, 6 Carry On, 12 Le Region

W. S. COX PLATE, *(Moonee Valley, 24/10/1931)*

Phar Lap 1st (9.4 *J. Pike*) .... **Chatham 2nd** .... **Johnnie Jason 3rd** .... Won by: 2½ len .... Time: 2:1½

FLEMINGTON

Saturday, October 31, 1931

MELBOURNE STAKES

(Weight-for-Age)
10 furlongs

1	*Phar Lap*		
	9.1	J. Pike	£525
2	*Concentrate*		
	9.1	A. Reed	£150
3	*Veilmond*		
	9.0	J. Munro	£75

WON BY
½ len, 1¼ len. Time: 2:6½

ALSO RAN

Cimbrian   9.4   O. Phillips   0

NO BETTING

MELBOURNE STAKES, *(Flemington, 31/10/1931)*

Phar Lap 1st *(9.1 J. Pike)* .... **Concentrate 2nd** .... **Veilmond 3rd** .... *Won by: ½ len* .... *Time: 2:6½*

AGUA CALIENTE

Mexico, Sunday, March 20, 1932

AGUA CALIENTE HANDICAP

10 furlongs

1	*Phar Lap*			
	9.3	.... W. Elliot		US$ 50,000
2	*Reveille Boy*			
	8.6	.... R. Wholey		US $5,000
3	*Scimitar*			
	7.2	.... G. Smith		US$2,500

WON BY

2 len, 2½ len. Time: 2:2.8 (Course record)

ALSO RAN

Joe Flores	6.6	*S. Coucci*	4
Marine	8.2	*F. Mann*	5
Good And Hot	7.2	*W. Moran*	6
Seth's Hope	8.0	*C. Turk*	7
Spanish Play	8.5	*C. Landolt*	8
Dr. Freeland	8.8	*L. Cunningham*	9
Bahamas	7.1	*J. Longden*	0
Cabezo	7.2	*A. Fischer*	0

BETTING (Agua Caliente Tote)

6/4 Phar Lap, 3 Spanish Play, 13/2 Joe Flores, Cabezo, 7 Reveille Boy, 10 Bahamas, 15 Dr. Freeland, 20 Marine, 30 Scimitar, 40 Seth's Hope, 60 Good And Hot

AGUA CALIENTE HCP, *(Agua Caliente, Mexico, 20/3/1932)*

Phar Lap 1st *(9.3 W. Elliot)* .... **Reveille Boy 2nd** .... *Scimitar 3rd* .... *Won by: 2 len* .... *Time: 2:2.8 (Course record)*

THE
PHAR LAP
COLLECTION